A Guide to Local Housing Needs Assessment

Valli van Zijl
David Couttie Associates Ltd

Institute of Housing

The Institute of Housing

The Institute of Housing is the professional organisation for all people who work in housing. Its purpose is to take a strategic and leading role in encouraging and promoting the provision of good quality affordable housing for all. The Institute has more than 11,000 members working in local authorities, housing associations, the private sector and educational institutions.

Institute of Housing
Octavia House
Westwood Way
Coventry CV4 8JP
Telephone: 0203 694433

A Guide to Local Housing Needs Assessment

Author: Valli van Zijl, David Couttie Associates Ltd
Editor: Jason MacGilp

Published by the Institute of Housing

ISBN 0 901607 70 3

Graphic design by Henry's House Design Co–operative Ltd.
Printed by Decor Profiles & Exhibitions Ltd

Contents

Acknowledgements

I would like to thank all the local authority personnel who responded to my request for examples of activities in housing needs assessment, many of which have been referred to in the Guide. However, the response was overwhelming and not all of them could be mentioned individually.

In particular, I would like to thank,
Malcolm Boorer, Llanelli Borough Council
Mike Stone, Hall and Tawse (ex New Forest District Council)
Hal Pawson, London Borough of Hackney
Stephen Oldridge, Ryedale District Council
John Kirk, Ashford Borough Council
Alan Brooks and Pat Cox, London Borough of Hammersmith and Fulham
Chris Jarvis, London Research Centre
Brian Leonard, Department of the Environment
Richard Wakeford, Department of the Environment
Jane Taylor, Housing Corporation
Michael Ashley, Association of District Council
for giving their time for detailed discussions and providing invaluable input to the Guide.

Thanks to the "readers,"
Mike Stones, Hall and Tawse
Morag McDermott, CATCH (ex Oxford City Council)
Bob Blackaby, Birmingham City Council
Patricia Hobbs, Leicester City Council
for reading and offering useful comments on the text.

I would particularly like to thank David Couttie, Managing Director of DCA Ltd for his constructive comments on the text and for providng a useful "sounding board" throughout the preparation of the Guide. I would also like to thank Jason MacGilp, Policy Officer at the Institute of Housing, for commissioning the publication and for his comments. A special thanks also to Dana Zalesinska of DCA Ltd for so patiently amending my drafts and preparing the final draft.

Chapter 1
Local Housing Needs Assessment – A Practical Guide

1.1 Local Authorities' Strategic Housing Role – An Introduction

Over the past decade, the Government has continued to reduce local authorities' role as providers of new social housing. The Department of the Environment's White Paper in 1987 (*Housing : The Government's Proposals*) was the major turning point. Its objective was that local authorities should adopt a more *strategic* role to replace the traditional activity of building new homes. The provision of social housing would be taken over by housing associations which had, hitherto, played a complementary and somewhat subsidiary role to local authorities as housing providers.

Indeed, current policies such as Large Scale Voluntary Transfers, Compulsory Competitive Tendering, Rents to Mortgages and continued encouragement of the Right to Buy point to a scenario in which local authorities may also lose their housing management role. Some twenty authorities have already transferred all their stock to housing associations. These local authorities now have, exclusively, a strategic and enabling role to perform.

In its White Paper *Housing – the First Priority* (June 1992), the Institute of Housing envisages that, where councils have very large stocks of housing, they may consider splitting the strategic and management roles. Management could be devolved to arms–length local housing companies accountable to the strategic centre.

However, whether local authorities have transferred their stock to a housing association or considered the option of setting up local housing companies, or whether they continue to be managers of housing does not detract from the importance of the strategic role and the need to formulate a comprehensive and wide ranging housing strategy to enable the housing needs in their area to be met.

The significant changes in housing policy over recent years have resulted in a greater number of potential partners being involved in housing provision – housing associations, private developers, voluntary organisations etc. In addition, there will be further demands on housing arising from the Community Care legislation. There is, therefore, broad agreement that a local authority's role as the strategic housing authority is of critical importance in meeting housing needs in their area.

It is worth noting that neither the enabling nor the strategic roles are new to local authorities. Housing departments have always performed these tasks in addition to development and management. However they now comprise a far more significant part of a local authority's duty as well as a more prominent and an increasingly complex one.

There has been considerable discussion about the *enabling* role of local authorities, but less so of the strategic role which is either seen as secondary to, or is confused with, the enabling role. The enabling role can be seen as the provision of assistance to providers of social housing via financial support, provision of local authority land or the use of planning powers to enable social housing to be provided (see *Working together in the 1990's*, Fraser, 1991 and *Planning for Affordable Housing*, Dunmore, 1992). The *strategic* role involves:

- identifying housing needs and demands
- identifying the resources and powers available to meet that need
- preparation of a housing strategy to meet housing need using the appropriate enabling powers and the resources likely to be available.
- bringing together the key players in the district
- implementing and monitoring the strategy.

Meeting housing need requires, in most cases, the supply of land. A local authority's strategic housing role is therefore particularly closely linked to the authority's planning role and must reflect and be reflected in, the authority's local or unitary development plan. The strategic role involves the authority taking a corporate view of housing, embracing liaison with the planning department as well as social services and other appropriate departments.

Another important element of the strategic role is for housing authorities to look beyond the local authority itself and encourage other organisations to come forward with information they may have on housing need and any contribution they can make to meeting housing need, and to co–ordinate these contributions. Such organisations would include social service departments, where they are located in a separate authority, district and regional health authorities, housing associations, the Housing Corporation / Tai Cymru / Scottish Homes, voluntary organisations and housebuilders.

A local authority's housing strategy must go beyond the housing strategy statements which have accompanied HIP bids in the past. They need to provide a framework to address *all* housing requirements in the area–social and sale, private and public, rent and owner occupation.

In order to perform effectively as a strategic housing authority, to formulate a *relevant* housing strategy on which to base decision making and to stand the best chance of tackling problems effectively, local authorities need to have a comprehensive picture of all the housing needs in their area. This should include the scale of need, as well as the type of housing required, what people can afford to pay, and projections of the likely housing requirement over the time period of strategic plans. Local authorities therefore need to undertake proper research into housing need.

1.2 The Guide

The purpose of this guide is to consider the issues included in carrying out assessments of housing requirements. It will examine why they need to be undertaken (the policy background), what such assessments entail and the various options/complementary exercises which can be undertaken. The Guide provides some good practice advice using case studies from authorities which have undertaken assessments of housing need in their area.

There are essentially two aspects of housing need assessment. The first relates to the requirements and circumstances of the people who are in need of a home or, indeed, an alternative home to the current one which no longer meets their requirements. It is concerned with what type of home they require, what they can afford, the location of the home and the overall scale of the resultant need. In other words, this means assessing 'rehousing' needs in their widest context (see *Developing Local Authority Housing Strategies*, Audit Commission, 1992).

The second element of assessment is that of the condition of the local authority *and* private sector stock. Although the stock condition needs are undoubtedly important, particularly in assessing the need for additional housing, this document is only concerned with rehousing or "people's needs". Assessment of stock condition is an altogether different subject to the housing requirements of individuals and requires separate guidance. This is an area on which the Department of the Environment are currently undertaking further work, following the English House Condition Survey 1991. The establishment of a best practice unit for assessment of stock condition is also being considered. Scottish Homes published their preliminary findings of their 1991 House Condition Survey for Scotland in February 1993, with the full report due in June 1993.

In addition to looking at the policy background and best–practice examples of assessing the housing requirements of the residents of a local authority, this Guide provides information on how the data obtained on housing need can be used to inform the authority's housing strategy. It also considers to whom the information on the identified need in the context of the strategy should be targeted, in order to ensure that the housing to be provided in the district, borough or city meets the needs which exist and are projected to arise in the foreseeable future.

The intention is not to offer a single definitive model. The Guide presents a variety of approaches and methodologies and discusses the range of information needs in rural and urban areas. The Guide emphasises the importance of the corporate approach and the potential for informing the planning process, option appraisal and the development of local housing strategies.

Development of Local Strategies

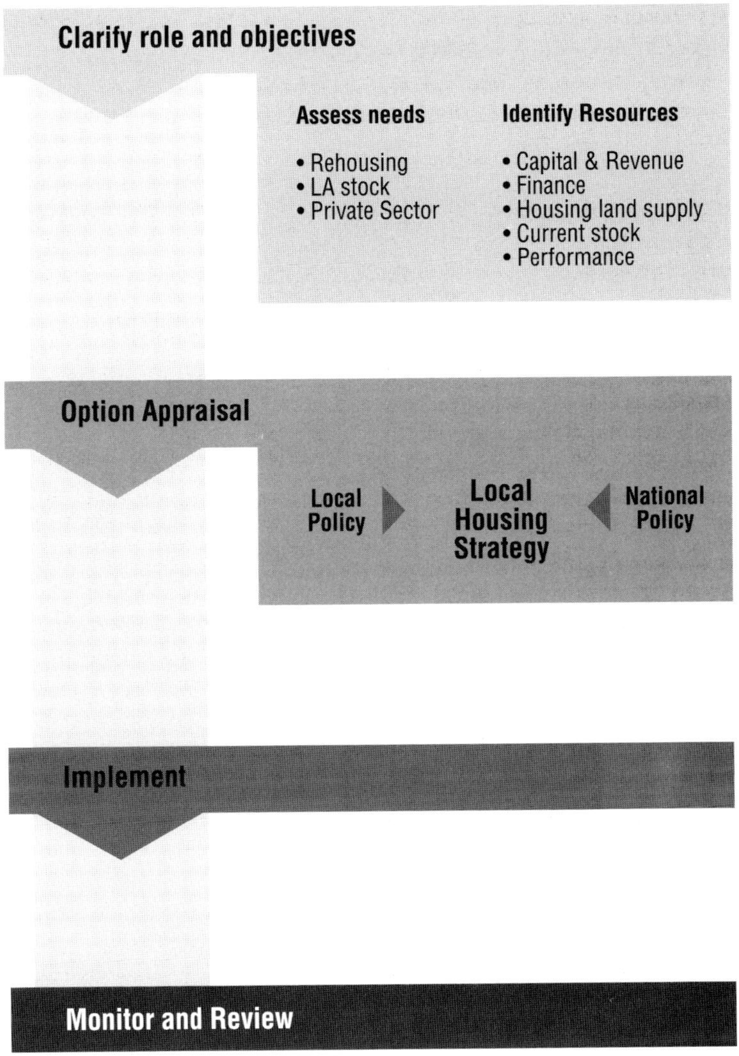

(adapted from Audit Commission, 1992).

Chapter 2

Why Assess Housing Need?

2.1 Introduction

The assessment of the need for housing in a district is the fundamental requirement for the formulation of a local authority's housing strategy. There are also other statutory reasons for assessment, as well as providing the local authority with information on which to base its enabling role. This chapter will look at the policy background to the assessment of housing need, including a brief glance back in housing history, and other supporting evidence for the value of such an activity to a local housing authority.

2.2 Housing Legislation and Guidance – A Brief History

2.2.1 Housing Act 1985

Section 8 of the Housing Act 1985, which relates to the main powers and duties of local authorities states that:

> *Every local housing authority shall consider housing conditions in their district and the needs of the district with respect to the provision of further housing accommodation.*

Section 1 of the Housing (Scotland) Act 1987 gives the same duty, and stresses that local authorities should work in partnership with housing associations to ensure that the supply of new social housing is properly targeted to meet local housing needs. This requirement to appraise housing need was contained in the Housing Act 1957, prior to the consolidation of housing legislation in the 1985 Act, but in fact dates back to the Housing Act 1935. Concern about the poor housing conditions of many living in overcrowded circumstances resulted in the 1935 Act defining the conditions where overcrowding existed and imposing a requirement on local authorities to survey the extent of overcrowding in their area and to prepare plans to provide sufficient accommodation to resolve the problem of overcrowding.

2.2.2 DoE's HIP Guidance to Local Authorities

Housing Investment Programmes were introduced in 1977 and raised the awareness of the importance of assessing needs objectively and comprehensively. The Department of Environment produced some guidance on information and techniques for assessing housing requirements in 1980, in which waiting lists were seen as a key source of information. Housing strategies and HIP statements were, until the recent guidance in 1992, confined to the housing needs for which the local authority had a statutory responsibility.

The HIP process in England and similarly the HSOP in Wales encouraged local authorities to undertake research into their local housing needs to provide a picture of the scale of the problem which needed to be tackled. However, this practice became less prevalent in the 1980s. The need for housing in most areas far outstripped supply and with the continuing decline in the number of public sector homes being built, local authorities were not able to do much more than house the homeless. There seemed little point in assessing need that they were unable to meet and raise expectations in the process.

The Government's White paper in 1987 *Housing: The Government's Proposals* described a strategic role for local authorities:

> *"The future role of local authorities will be a strategic one – identifying housing needs and demands, and encouraging innovative methods of provision by other bodies to meet these needs..."*

Subsequent HIP guidance notes, particularly those for the 1990 and 1991 HIP rounds, gave details on local authorities' enabling role. The 1992 guidance to local authorities on the HIP round stresses the vital role local authorities have to play as housing enablers and strategic housing authorities and that strategies should encompass *all* the housing needs of an area.

As local authorities are no longer the providers of the majority of new rented housing in their area, and with increasing emphasis on their strategic and enabling roles, local authorities need to identify all housing needs, whether they be for sale or social housing. It has become even more important to provide those now delivering housing with information on housing need to ensure that priority needs are met. Such information could also be used to inform providers who may be able to meet a need for shared ownership or sale housing at the lower end of the market, and by planners to ensure that sufficient land is available for the sale and social housing required.

2.2.3 1992 HIP and HSOP Guidance Round

The 1992 HIP Guidance states that strategies

- will be expected to cover needs and resources on an informed and realistic basis
- will be informed by reliable data and analysis of the housing needs of the area... Authorities should draw on any appropriate source of information and, where necessary, should undertake their own surveys and studies.

Similarly, the Welsh Office guidance *Housing Strategies and Operational Plans for 1993/94 to 1995/6*, states that strategies should be based on a broad, prioritised assessment of housing requirements in the district. Local authorities are also referred to the Audit Commission guidance (1992) regarding the need for local authorities to consider needs by client group, not simply by tenure. The Welsh Office guidance highlights the importance of assessing the extent to which housing needs can be met through the open market.

The importance of a comprehensive picture of housing need to inform a housing strategy is implicit in the Welsh Office guidance. Local authorities which include HSOP's are expected to perform a number of functions:

- to inform and influence the activities of other agencies in the housing field in the authority's area;

- to assist the Department in establishing where capital resources not distributed by formula can be most effectively spent.

These objectives require a detailed knowledge of all housing needs in the local authority's area. Central government is looking for local authorities to have evidence of need which should inform their strategy and resource bids.

2.2.4 *Allocation by Discretion*

For 1992/93, 60% of housing resources in England (Annual Capital Guidelines) have been allocated by discretion and 40% by the Generalised Needs Index. The Government has indicated that the use of discretion may well increase in future years. In Wales there is no "discretionary" element. Housing resources are allocated according to the GNI score of local authorities. In using their discretion, Ministers (in England) will take account of a number of criteria, including:

- Relative housing needs;

- Efficiency and effectiveness of authorities.

2.2.5 *Relative Need*

The DoE argues that, although the "GNI–factor" has been reduced, need is still an important factor which Ministers will take into account when exercising their discretion. What they will be looking for is evidence of "relative" need. The GNI is not considered by the DoE and others fully to reflect factors of relative need at the local level. A review of the GNI is to be undertaken which has been welcomed as many believe improvement of the indicator is necessary for it to act as an accurate determinant of need. Nevertheless, the DoE still believe that the GNI should not be the only consideration when allocating resources. The discretionary element will take into account "relative need" which includes needs which:

- have recently arisen
- are not otherwise adequately covered by the GNI
- are more qualitative than quantitative
- reflect particular local stock condition.

Where a local authority has undertaken a housing survey or carried out a particular study which reveals a need, for example, for special needs housing, this evidence of relative need can be used to argue the authority's case for an increased allocation of the HIP resources in that region. If there is no hard evidence, the DoE is not likely to treat the request seriously.

2.2.6 'No Single Recipe'

The DoE Guidance note gives some information on the criteria which will be taken into account in the assessment of the efficiency and effectiveness of local authorities' housing investment programmes. Among other factors, authorities will be expected to demonstrate the need for new social housing investment. This evidence is expected to comprise of demographic data and special needs requirements, as well as stock condition and resources.

Although neither the DoE nor the Welsh Office specify a particular method of such assessments, considerable weight is being placed by Government on needs assessments when reviewing the implementation and effectiveness of the local housing strategy. An assessment of need provides the local authority with information to inform its strategy, for example, whether to concentrate on repairing its own stock or to allocate funds in support of newbuild activity.

Some local authorities having undertaken surveys have apparently been rewarded by increased HIP allocations, although it is difficult to attribute such increases to one activity. The local authority may also have disposed of land at a discount to housing associations or made use of its planning powers, which are all looked upon favourably by the Department. Nevertheless local authorities who have hard evidence of the housing need in their area, from surveys, studies and research, will meet one of the criteria laid down by the Department which they will take into account in the distribution of funds for housing.

Ministers recognise that circumstances may vary considerably between authorities. Every authority will not be expected to act in the same way in assessing needs or in performing the enabling role. Local authorities must set the activities they undertake in assessing need in the context of the information already available to them. If a local authority decides not to undertake a particular type of study or survey, they need to explain that they have considered this course of action, why they have rejected it, perhaps in the context of the local circumstances and the demand on available resources, and why an alternative method was more appropriate.

2.3 Planning and Affordable Housing

Radical changes have been made to the planning system in the last few years, in relation to affordable housing. The "exceptions" policy, applicable in rural areas, and the more recent powers for local authorities to set targets for the total amount of affordable housing required in the district as detailed in Planning Policy Guidance Note 3 (DoE and Welsh Office) are discussed in more detail in *Planning for Affordable Housing*, (Dunmore K, IoH & HBF, 1992). There is therefore a much closer link than previously between affordable housing and the planning system. However, the planning system alone cannot be expected to deliver affordable housing nor should it be seen as the primary vehicle for delivery.

Until the announcement of the "exceptions"policy in 1989, planning legislation emphasised that the planning system should be concerned with the land use and not the user. There were exceptions to the rule, however, such as dwellings for agricultural and key workers. The changes contained in the Planning Policy Guidance Note 3 (PPG3) now extend the planning system's influence to "local housing need". Whereas the planning system cannot stipulate the tenure, price or ownership of the housing that is required, planning controls can restrict occupation for example to local need as defined in the authority's policy on affordable housing in the development plan.

Implementation of both the "exceptions" policy and the affordable housing policy for mixed tenure developments require evidence of housing need. According to PPG3:

- new housing developments, where appropriate, should incorporate a mix and balance of house types and sizes to cater for a range of needs;

- where there is a *demonstrable* lack of affordable housing to meet local needs, local authorities may indicate an overall target for the provision of affordable housing throughout the plan area *based on evidence of need*;

- targets may be set for specific sites based on evidence of need and site suitability.

PPG3 contains an entire annex on *Affordable housing for local needs in rural areas* of which a substantial section is on "Assessing Needs" which states that local authorities will be expected to justify the adoption of low cost housing policies in their local plans *with clear evidence of local need.*

There has been some confusion regarding the implementation of PPG3 relating to planning conditions, finance and the assessment of need. This has led the Department of Environment to produce a consultation paper: *Draft Explanatory Note on Planning and Affordable Housing*. This Note stresses the need for local authorities to assess the need for affordable housing which should inform their local plans. In the negotiations with developers for an element of affordable housing, all the partners need to take account of:

- the extent of need
- the state of the local housing market and
- the availability of financial resources.

Evidence of the extent, and nature of the local need will, in the first instance, strengthen the local authority's bargaining position in these negotiations. Robust data is crucial for the authority's affordable housing policy to withstand an appeal by the developer.

2.4 Housing and Community Care

The assessment of need for supported housing or other housing for specific needs groups has been somewhat neglected by both housing and care providers. The increase in the number of homeless families that local authorities have a statutory responsibility to house has meant that special needs have had difficulty in competing for the limited funding available. The quest for value for money in the provision of new housing also mitigates against greater provision for this sector, even allowing for Special Needs Management Allowance (SNMA).

The NHS and Community Care Act 1990 and the joint Department of the Environment and Department of Health Circular (DoE 10/92) provide a further stimulus for the assessment of the need for supported housing:

> *"Adequate housing has a major role to play in community care and is often the key to independent living."*

Social services departments, as from April 1993, are required to assess the community care needs of their local population – including housing needs. Close co–operation between housing authorities and social services authorities on assessing needs and in the planning process is suggested as the way forward.

The Welsh office HSOP Guidance (1992) advises local authorities in preparing their housing strategies and operational plans to *"give due recognition to the housing needs in their area in relation to community care working with social services authorities, health authorities, Tai Cymru, housing associations and other relevant bodies."* This is likely to require an assessment of housing need in the area for future years arising from community care and other special needs. The objective of community care is to enable people to remain in their existing housing where they choose to do so and where it is both possible and cost effective. This may require care and support or it may require some adaptation to the dwelling, or both. Information on such housing need and its scale will inform the housing authority's housing strategy and provide hard evidence to support the authority's bid for renovation grants, "minor works assistance" and Disabled Facilities Grants.

However, in some cases alternative accommodation will be required. The closure of long stay hospitals, for example, will necessitate the provision of homes in the community for the people hitherto housed in these institutions. Additional homes will also need to be provided for people who cannot remain in their own homes, even with support, and for people who no longer want to remain in the family home, but would prefer some level of independent living.

With a complete picture of the need for supported housing, local authorities can hold informed discussions with housing associations, the Housing Corporation, Tai Cymru and Scottish Homes to ensure that the needs of all priority groups are addressed. Good quality information will enable authorities to bring greater pressure to bear on the allocation of funding in their favour.

2.5 Housing Corporation, Tai Cymru and Housing Associations

The Housing Corporation's stated objective is to maximise housing provision to address local housing needs. The allocation of funding to schemes put forward by housing associations is said to be needs–led, with the priority needs for the area being defined, annually, with the local authority. In each region of the Corporation, at least 50% of the rented programme must be used to provide homes for homeless households. In practice most regions are exceeding this proportion. The remaining element of the programme is allocated according to other priorities identified by the authority.

Tai Cymru's *Investment Policies and Plan 1992/93* document states that in order to meet the objective of *"increasing the supply of well managed, good quality housing for those unable to meet their housing needs through purchase or rental at open market prices"* they need to ensure that all resources are well targeted. (Tai Cymru, 1992/93).

Both Tai Cymru and the Housing Corporation evaluate the strategies and priorities for each local authority, annually, which includes determining the housing needs and priorities in discussion with the local authority.

Tai Cymru is, however, concerned about the inconsistency of the quality of information on housing need across Wales and by the continued use of waiting lists as primary indicators of need. This is a particular worry in rural areas where inadequate information on housing needs could result in investment not addressing the greatest housing need.

Without a comprehensive view of the housing need in their area, local authorities could be neglecting certain people who could be helped, for example, by shared ownership, and could be missing out on possible "additional" funding for special needs housing as 13% of each region's programme is earmarked for such schemes. With resources for such schemes falling well short of the need, the limited money is likely to go to those authorities who have identified particular needs and formulated strategies for meeting as much of this need as possible. In support of this, the following policy statements may be cited (see *Community Care Planning: A Model for Housing Need Assessment*, Harker/Watson, IoH & NFHA,1993):

- *Local authorities are expected to assess the local need for shared ownership and to have taken account of this in their housing strategies;*

housing for both key workers and first–time buyers can be funded in this way.
Policy Statement 1993/94, Housing Corporation
East Midlands Region

- *The Region will consider bids for other special needs groups where such a project receives high priority from a local authority (including a social services authority), or where a significant deficiency in provision can be demonstrated.*
  Policy Statement 1993/94, Housing Corporation
  London and Home Counties (North East) Region

80% of each English region's programme is allocated to local authorities on the basis of their HNI scores, and 70% in Wales. The remainder will be distributed at the discretion of the Regional Offices of the Housing Corporation and Tai Cymru, in Wales. Given the government's intention to synchronize the HIP/HSOP and Annual Development Programmes (ADP) processes, the criteria which the Corporation and Tai Cymru will consider in allocating their discretionary element are much the same as those used by the DoE. They are likely to take account of each local authority's performance in their role as housing enablers, including the assessment of need. For instance, the East Midlands Region of the Housing Corporation in assessing a local authority's performance, considers a local housing strategy must seek to

identify, quantify and prioritise the broad spectrum of housing needs (i.e. not just statutory responsibilities and waiting lists).
Policy Statement 1993/4

Tai Cymru give no guarantee that each local authority's allocation will be exactly in line with the HNI score. The remaining 30% will enable Tai Cymru to react to acute needs which have arisen since the HNI was set. Another reason for the 30% "discretion" element is that the HNI does not contain specific measurement of need for housing for people with special care or support needs. The allocation of this 30% is based on commissioned data, local circumstances and knowledge. Assessment of need by local authorities which highlight a particular local problem are therefore likely to prove most useful in negotiations with both Tai Cymru and the Housing Corporation regarding allocations.

2.6 Housing Need in Scotland

2.6.1 Housing Plans

The assessment of housing need has also been central to the formulation of Housing Plans in Scotland since the late 1970's. In 1977 the Scottish Development Department published a Scottish Housing Handbook on assessing housing needs (SDD 1977) to "provide guidance for officials of local authorities in preparing comprehensive assessments of housing needs in their areas" which is still largely relevant to assessing needs today. The SDD had addressed the issue of assessing need as early as 1972 when it produced a document called *Planning for Housing Needs; pointers towards a comprehensive approach* (SDD).

In their Housing Plans local authorities are asked to assess the overall housing needs of their areas and set out medium term strategies for meeting these needs. The allocation of funding to individual local authorities takes account of the information on relative housing need. According to the Scottish Office's consultation paper *(Housing Plans, Programmes and Capital Allocations*, 1992*)* the quality of their Housing Plans and the effectiveness and efficiency with which authorities use the resources available to them will be an increasingly important factor. Greater emphasis is to be placed on the need for authorities to take a strategic overview of all housing needs in their area. The Scottish Office are concerned, amongst other issues, that a rigorous discussion of priorities is often absent from Housing Plans. Comprehensive assessments of housing need will clearly address these concerns and funding criteria.

The Consultation paper states that

> *local authorities should continue to take the lead in their strategic and enabling role, in assessing overall local housing needs in their areas and developing strategies designed to meet these needs.*
> *(Scottish Office, October 1992)*

The Scottish Office is also concerned that Housing Plans should be based on a realistic view of resource availability, although others have argued that unless the Plans are needs led, the Government will not be aware of what the scale of the need actually is in order to set a realistic national budget for investment in housing. However, the consultation paper states that authorities "would of course be free" to demonstrate that additional need exists which will not be met by the resources likely to be allocated, and should state how these needs would be met were additional resources made available. Housing needs assessments would be useful in this regard as they provide robust information on need.

2.6.2 Planning and Affordable Housing

The relationship between planning and affordable housing in Scotland is at a different stage of development from that prevailing in England and Wales in that the National Planning Policy Guidance (NPPG 1), *Land for Housing* (1991) is still in draft form. Nevertheless, the guidance given to planning authorities regarding low cost housing is confined to a section on low cost housing for local needs in *rural* areas. It states that

> *A community's need for low cost housing is therefore a matter which may properly be taken into account in formulating development plan policies.*

It stresses that liaison with the housing authority, who will be responsible for quantifying the need for low cost housing for local needs in its areas, and Scottish Homes, is vital. Where a lack of low cost housing is demonstrated, local plans can include policies indicating the intention to negotiate with developers to include a "quota of low cost housing for local needs in new housing developments of reasonable size".

Local authorities may also "zone exceptionally" sites for low cost housing which would not normally be allocated for housing within or adjoining a village. The assessment of local need is therefore important in implementing such low cost housing policies, yet the guidance states that there is no fixed set of national criteria for assessing need. Much, it continues, will depend on local housing circumstances and needs.

2.6.3 Scottish Homes

Scottish Homes, as the national housing agency for Scotland, has as it broad aim to ensure that the quality and variety of housing options available to people of Scotland are substantially improved. In order to achieve this aim it works closely with others including local authorities. Over half the local authorities in Scotland have now concluded strategic investment agreements with Scottish Homes, which aim to set out a framework for addressing housing provision in partnership and to establish local priorities for investment.

Scottish Homes is also involved in helping to improve assumptions and information about the assessment of local housing needs and the quality of local housing market information generally. Given the different housing profile, and the even more determined push by the government to increase owner occupation in Scotland (where the proportion of owner occupiers is 51% compared to 67% in England), the emphasis in assessing housing needs is somewhat different. Scottish Homes has co–sponsored *Local Market Analyses* in a number of local authorities. It has recently commissioned the Centre for Housing Research, Glasgow University to produce good practice guidance (1993) for local market analyses and needs assessments which is intended to provide a district level strategic planning tool. This has entailed a considerable amount of research and a number of case studies, providing comprehensive information on local market analyses.

This guide will not attempt to cover this form of assessment although it is hoped that the information contained will be of interest and assistance to all local authorities in Scotland, England and Wales.

2.7 Priority Investment Areas

Evidence of need for shared–ownership schemes can make a considerable impact in the actual affordability of shared–ownership. The Housing Corporation's Procedure Guidance states that the definition of Priority Investment Areas (PIAs) will be

> *"areas specifically identified in the Regional Policy Statement where the local authority needs assessment has demonstrated a requirement for low cost housing for sale"*.
> (Volume III – *Housing for Sale*).

In PIA's the Low–Cost Home Ownership (LCHO) factor for the calculation of grant is 58%, compared to 50% in non–PIA's.

A housing needs assessment which identifies a need for shared ownership would help make a strong case to the Housing Corporation to classify the local authority as a PIA, or to effectively reclassify, as was the case in

London and Home Counties (NE) Region where ultimately around 90% of authorities in the region were granted PIA status.

2.8 Social Housing Agreements

In England, the National Federation of Housing Associations, together with the Association of District Councils and the Association of Metropolitan Authorities have prepared a paper proposing the drawing up of social housing agreements between housing associations and local authorities at local level. Given the significant changes in the government's expectations of both local authorities and housing associations, an agreement between the parties which clarifies the respective roles and relationships is seen as offering a useful framework for the provision of social housing.

The NFHA/ADC/AMA paper lists the likely duties of the parties concerned. The first task included in the local authority's strategic role is *assessing local housing needs*.

Local authorities and housing associations would be expected to involve the Housing Corporation at local level in discussions regarding the objectives of the social housing agreements and the resources likely to be made available to implement them. In Wales and Scotland, Tai Cymru and Scottish Homes are entering into Strategic Housing Agreements with local authorities. The purpose of these agreements is to further the working relationship with local authorities and to provide a more formal basis for partnership. Tai Cymru have stressed the need to increase awareness of the importance of the strategic responsibilities of local authorities including the assessment of need.

2.9 Other Reasons for Needs Assessments

Apart from the requirement by central government, and others, to undertake comprehensive needs assessments, there are a number of other reasons for so doing. These include:

- provision of information to assist in prioritising schemes, both by type of housing, need and location

- definitive evidence of housing need which can help persuade various parties (e.g. planners, planning committee, Housing Corporation/Tai Cymru/Scottish Homes, central government, parish councils) of the housing problem in the area

- strengthening of the local authority's bargaining position regarding investment for housing and inclusion of low–cost and social housing in residential development

- if publicised, information gathered can help to raise the profile of housing, both locally and nationally. With central government's reluctance to undertake its own national needs assessment (or to endorse the widely accepted 100,000 new units of social housing per annum) local housing needs assessments help to emphasise the importance of, and support for the case for, greater investment in housing at a national level.

2.10 The Value of Local Needs Assessments – A Summary

Direct Benefits

- Objective assessments to inform investment decisions.

- Encourage active option appraisal.

- Provide basis for bids for capital resources and initiatives.

- Provide new range of information.

- Provide solid base for Local Housing Strategy.

- Give focus to enabling role.

Indirect Benefits:

- Encourage a comprehensive, corporate approach.
- Contribute to wider social/economic strategies.
- Increase profile of housing issues.
- Provide focus for liaison with other agencies.
- Identify areas for improved efficiency.

Chapter 3
How Are Housing Needs Assessed?

3.1 Introduction

This chapter considers the type of information required and considers the range of sources which could contribute to this database, as it is unlikely that any one source will provide a comprehensive picture. It takes a critical look at waiting lists in particular and suggests other alternative sources which are dealt with in more detail in subsequent chapters

3.2 What information is required?

Housing strategies of the 1990s are required to be wide ranging in that they must address all the housing need in the local authority area. Local authorities must do all they can to ensure that the appropriate housing is provided to meet these varied needs. The assessment of need must be as comprehensive as possible and must include the need for social rented housing; shared ownership and sale housing, specifically adapted housing and adaptations to existing accommodation. Housing need assessments should not be confined to the requirement for new dwellings.

When considering the assessment of need in their area local authorities may consider the starting point to be a definition of housing need. However, this can be limiting as authorities may define needs in terms of their statutory responsibilities. This would reduce the scope of the assessment of need and thereby ignore groups for whom the local authority has no responsibility but who may equally be in housing need. This need could be addressed by other agencies.

In considering undertaking an assessment of need the local authority must encompass the entire housing spectrum in its locality, so as to obtain as much information on the need for housing as possible. Analysis of the data collected will provide information on various areas of housing need which the local authority will then be in a position to use to make a case to the Government for funding, or propose ways in which other organisations can assist (eg the provision of shared ownership using discounted land via the planning system).

Furthermore, information merely on the overall scale of housing need is insufficient as those in need are not one homogeneous mass, but have particular requirements and aspirations which must also be considered. Information must be obtained on a number of aspects including the type of accommodation required, the size of dwelling, the preferred locality and tenure, any necessary adaptations and must be related to what people can actually afford.

As housing strategies are required to cover a three year period, and the timespan of local authority local plans is, usually, ten years, they must be informed by projections of housing need.

3.3 Waiting Lists as a Source of Information

In guidance produced some time ago by the Scottish Development Department (1976) and the Department of the Environment (1980) on assessing housing requirements, waiting lists are suggested as a key source for obtaining information on housing need. However, although waiting lists may have some value as databases providing information on, for example, incidence of overcrowding and can be useful as an indication of housing need in the absence on any other measure, it is doubtful that they are of significant use as an overall measure of housing need.

The Audit Commission's report (1992) states that "Waiting lists do not paint a comprehensive picture particularly in areas of housing shortage". Housing is likely to be required by those ineligible for acceptance onto the council's housing waiting list eg. single people, under 18 (though hopefully the Children Act may address this issue in England and Wales), and people on relatively high incomes but who are still not able to purchase or rent on the open market.

Research commissioned by the Department of the Environment (1988) into waiting lists revealed a high degree of inaccuracy. This research revealed that waiting lists often include names of large numbers of people who no longer consider themselves to be in housing need. In addition, not everyone who registers is in immediate housing need. Some double counting is also likely if the number of households on local housing associations' waiting lists are simply added to the local authority's list, as people in need of housing may, understandably, try every available option. No record is kept of those who do not qualify.

The DoE research led the London Evening Standard to claim that

> *"The Nation's housing crisis is not half as serious as statistics would have us believe."*

This, however, is only part of the story. The DoE study looked at waiting lists only. It did not consider the need that was not identified by waiting lists. Household surveys have revealed an underestimation of need far greater in scale than the overestimation suggested by DoE. For example, the London Housing Survey (1986/7) revealed that, whereas there were 127,000 households registered on waiting lists, there were in fact 280,000 households in measurable housing need and a further 250,000 hidden households living as part of another household.

A district wide household survey of Ryedale District in North Yorkshire showed a similar underestimation. Responses showed 78% of potential new households requiring accommodation were not registered on a waiting list. Recent research undertaken by the Scottish office has also concluded that local authority housing waiting lists were not good indicators of housing need.

There has undeniably been a decline in the importance of the waiting list as an "access" channel to social housing as homelessness figures increase and take priority, to varying degrees, over waiting lists. Some local authorities have set allocation quotas for the various groups such as waiting list applicants, homeless households, transfers, rehousing agreements and rehousing due to redevelopment. Because such a small proportion of households on the waiting list in any authority are housed, people are deterred from applying. The existence of a correlation between the likelihood of being rehoused and the rate of applications to a waiting list is borne out by DoE research which found a tendency for local authorities with smaller housing stock relative to the population to have relatively shorter waiting lists.

Rural areas have witnessed a marked reduction in the ability of local authorities to house local people largely as a result of the Right to Buy with no replacement of the stock. This factor coupled with the increase in house prices in the 1980's which pushed houses out of reach of local people living and working in rural areas, increased the need for social housing substantially but was not reflected in local authorities' waiting lists. The rural communities, to various degrees across the country, were galvanised into identifying the need for housing. Parish councils, with the assistance and/or encouragement of Rural Community Councils, undertook local surveys to raise awareness of the need for social housing in rural areas (see Chapter 5).

Waiting lists alone do not provide a comprehensive measure of the need for housing, but are a means of allocating available housing to those in need. In addition, where local authorities are unable to repeat other assessment exercises (eg. surveys) as frequently as may be wished, waiting lists can provide a means of updating the available information on need.

3.4 Enhanced Indicators of Need

The usefulness of waiting lists can be enhanced by a number of measures. The following are some suggestions which local authorities may have already considered or implemented:

- Regular updating
- "Waiting list" publicised as a register of need
- Less restrictive eligibility criteria so as to obtain a broader picture of need
- Inclusion of information on income
- Inclusion of information about disabilities/hold a disability register (eg Suffolk Districts, Gillingham Borough Council)
- Maintaining a separate shared ownership register (eg Chichester District Council) which would need to be publicised to the wider population (ie not only local authority tenants).
- Common waiting list and application form (eg Wrekin District Council, East Northamptonshire District Council).

Even if improvements to waiting lists are made, they alone will be unable to provide a complete picture of the housing situation in a local authority area. As strategic housing authorities, local authorities need to be aware of all housing need, even if it is not able to offer rehousing itself. Local authorities should be in a position to inform other providers who may be able to meet some of the need.

Thus local authorities need to look beyond the waiting list and homelessness information. Although there may be some truth in the allegation that identifying need raises the expectations without the ability to address it, housing authorities have to identify need both to allow possible options to be considered and to make a case to Government to increase funding for housing. The Government refuses to put a figure on need nationally. Local authorities, by assessing the widest requirement for housing, will be able to show the Government the scale of funding required.

3.5 Other Sources of Information on Housing Need

Household surveys
Household surveys offer one means of obtaining hitherto unavailable information on housing circumstances and the need for housing. (See Chapter 4)

Special needs surveys
In order to obtain a more detailed picture of special needs, a dedicated survey can be undertaken. (See Chapter 6)

Secondary data
A housing strategy needs to be informed by an overall view of the housing situation, which should include information on an area basis including the size of the population, their housing conditions, the likely future growth in the number and the type of households. (See Chapter 8)

The local housing market
Analysis of the local housing market can be undertaken in terms of house prices, market rents and incomes, providing information on local affordability. (See Chapter 7)

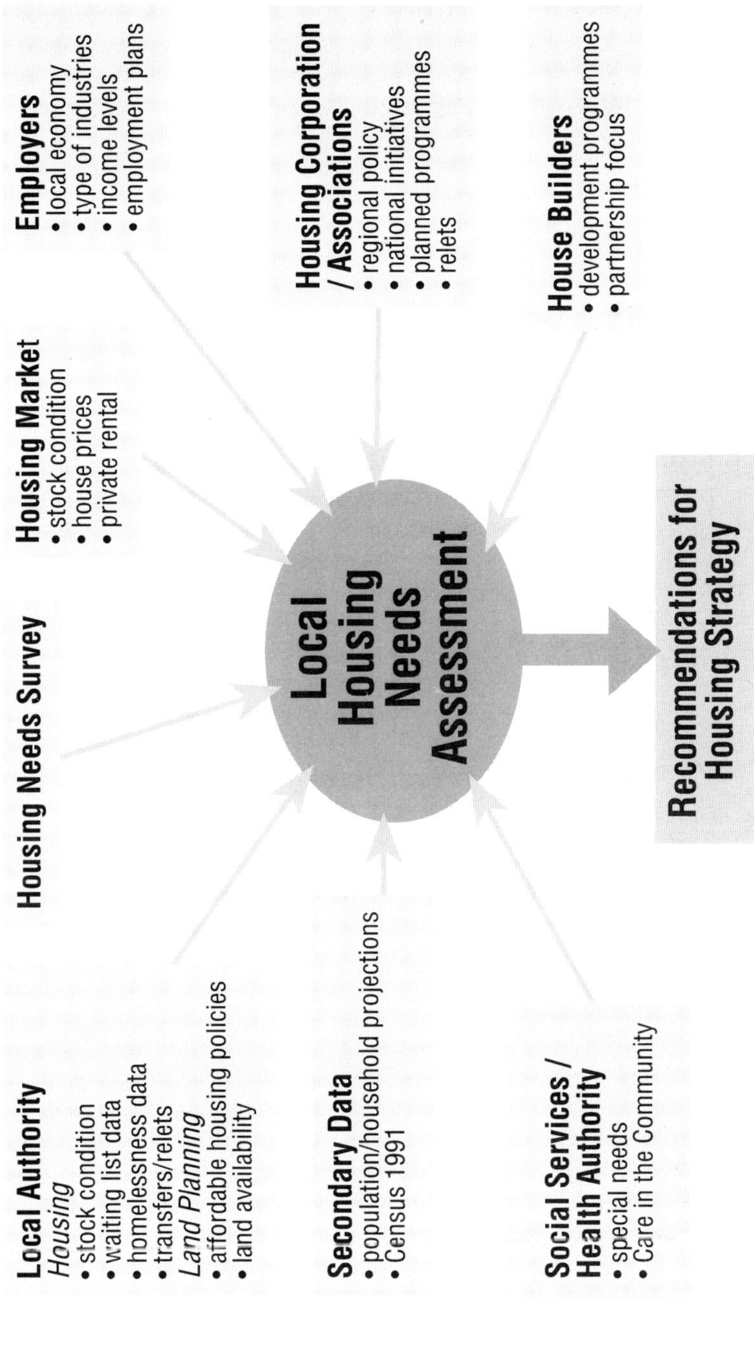
Local Authority
Housing
• stock condition
• waiting list data
• homelessness data
• transfers/relets
Land Planning
• affordable housing policies
• land availability
Housing Needs Survey
Housing Market
• stock condition
• house prices
• private rental
Employers
• local economy
• type of industries
• income levels
• employment plans
Secondary Data
• population/household projections
• Census 1991
Local Housing Needs Assessment
Housing Corporation / Associations
• regional policy
• national initiatives
• planned programmes
• relets
Social Services / Health Authority
• special needs
• Care in the Community
House Builders
• development programmes
• partnership focus
Recommendations for Housing Strategy

Chapter 4
Housing Need Surveys

4.1 Introduction

The inadequacy of waiting lists has led to local authorities and others undertaking housing need surveys to obtain a comprehensive picture of housing need. This chapter looks at what is involved in such a survey and some of the options which should be considered when embarking on such a project. It does not attempt to provide a definitive guide to housing needs surveys, market research or statistics, but raises some of the issues most likely to be confronted in embarking on a housing needs survey.

A number of case studies are dealt with in some detail to illustrate the various options, reasons for undertaking surveys and use of information obtained.

4.2 What does a Household Survey entail?

4.2.1 Setting objectives

The objectives of a survey must be clearly spelt out and understood from the outset. Housing and planning departments may have individual reasons for undertaking a survey, requiring slightly different information. This should be clear before work commences on the survey, so that their respective requirements can be addressed.

This therefore requires consultation between all departments who are likely to make use of the survey information in policy and strategy preparation. This includes social services (whether in the same unitary authority or in the County Council) as well as planning and housing.

Outside agencies, such as housing associations, housebuilders and voluntary organisations should also be consulted to ensure their concerns are addressed and the information to be collected enables them to prepare their strategies.

What does a survey entail?

- determining what information is required and from whom
- designing and selecting the sample
- translating the information required into a survey questionnaire
- piloting the survey ie testing the adequacy of the questionnaire and other aspects of the survey design
- carrying out the field work for the main survey
- editing, processing and tabulating survey forms
- analysing the results

4.2.2 Preparation of a brief

Whether the local authority itself intends to undertake the survey or some part of it, it is advisable to draw up as comprehensive a brief as possible, taking account of the discussions with the various departments and other organisations mentioned above.

The brief should:

- Provide some background information on the housing strategy and the local plan with regard to any affordable housing policy (that is assuming the survey is to serve both a housing and a planning purpose)

- Give, in some detail, the aims of the survey ie. the type of information the Council requires.

- Give some indication of the use to which the council intends to put the information gathered.

If the council has well–founded preferences about the methodology to be adopted, these should be laid out in the brief. However, where authorities do not have a dedicated research department or team, it is advisable that the final decisions about methodology are left to the consultants who will undertake the survey

Case Study
Rugby Borough Council

Rugby Borough Council, who have recently put a Housing Needs Survey out to tender, prepared an informative brief providing the consultants with a clear idea of the purpose of the survey and the areas to be covered. A copy of the Housing Strategy Statement and form HIP 1 were attached, as were copies of the affordable housing policies contained in the Draft Local plan.

Background Information on:

- the size, population and population spread of the borough
- the housing strategy and local plan.

Aims of the Survey

"Information is required on the unmet housing need in the Borough so that the Council can implement its Housing and Planning policies –this information includes the need for housing by type of property, household and tenure as well as the overall scale; the scale of immediate need, need over the next five years and over the next 5–10 year period; the need for specialist accommodation; the housing aspirations of emerging households and how well the housing waiting list accurately reflects need."

The Council also requested information on the supply of low cost home ownership and rented accommodation; the relationship of income data to house prices and rent levels.

Methodology

It has been left to the tenderers to submit details of the methodology they intend to adopt. However the Council will need to be satisfied that the appropriate target groups in the population will be reached; the survey will be properly administered ; appropriate methods will be used to ensure a high level of response and that a high level of statistical confidence will result.

The brief also specifies the computer software used in the Council and states that the information gathered should be transferable to the Council's computers

Use of data

This section covers, briefly, the HIP submission timetable and the local plan timetable and states that the tenderers should be prepared to appear at the Local Plan Inquiry to support the information produced by the survey.

4.3 Choosing Categories of Information / Questions to be asked

This will depend on the use to which the information is to be put as well as the availability of other up–to–date information and should involve close liaison between client and consultant.

4.3.1 Census Data

For example the 1991 Census provides relatively up to date information on tenure, sharing amenities etc (see Chapter 8). Therefore there is little point in repeating Census type questions to gather data already available and using valuable space on the questionnaire. However, a household survey carried out a few years hence, towards the mid– and late 1990s may need to revisit some of the Census topics to provide an update. Some Census type information (eg household composition, tenure etc.) is necessary for cross tabulation of other information.

4.3.2 New Information

Surveys are a means of obtaining information that is not available elsewhere and it is this information which surveys should concentrate on eg. special needs; need for alternative accommodation or adaptation; adequacy of accommodation–too large, too small, requires essential repair etc;whether household intends to move in given period and if so why; cost of housing; attitude to further housing development in town/village, to meet a particular need; whether any members of the household had left the town/village/area because of the lack of affordable housing or other reasons. Information on people's aspirations, attitudes and intentions is not available from any other source. This should therefore form a key part of any survey questionnaire.

In particular, household surveys enable information to be obtained on potential households, ie. concealed households which are living as part of another household but who wish to form a separate household of their own, accommodation permitting. A survey can enquire as to:

- the presence of hidden households currently looking for accommodation
- households likely to be looking for accommodation in the next three years
- potential households likely to require housing within 3 or 5 years

Housing needs are so fluid that to enquire about likely need beyond 3 or 5 years will not produce reliable data.

A separate section, or a separate questionnaire, can be devoted to these potential households to enquire about the size of household, ethnic origin, when the accommodation is required, what type of accommodation is required, special needs, tenure preference, preferred location and reason for preference, as well as the maximum amount the household is prepared to pay for accommodation and the household income.

4.3.3 Income

Income is a sensitive area to question but asking respondents to choose an income band (eg £10,000 – £12,000) can increase the response rate.

Case Study
East Hampshire District Council

East Hampshire District Council undertook a District wide Housing Need Survey in 1991. They decided not to ask an income question in their survey owing to the sensitivity of the subject which might reduce the response rate to the survey as a whole. When reviewing the survey they decided that information on income would have been most useful and would certainly include a question on household income in any future update of the survey.

50% of the respondents to a housing need survey completed the question on incomes, which involved choosing an income band rather than having to specify their actual income. This provided invaluable data on local incomes.

The income question is one which lends itself better to an interview–type questionnaire (see below for postal vs interview critique); this is not necessarily because a respondent may be less likely to give an interviewer false information than indicate the wrong band on a form. It is more due to the fact that the interviewer can probe the interviewee regarding, for example, overtime and bonuses which could either be ignored or over/under estimated on a self–completion form and which will take up a considerable amount of the space on the questionnaire if requested for every working individual.

It is easier to ignore a section on income when completing it oneself than when being interviewed. In addition, the interviewer can make some judgements about the accuracy or otherwise of the given household income when in the home, which cannot be done by postal questionnaires. Income information from postal questionnaires should not be disregarded altogether, but should be treated with caution. It could be useful to compare it with other (County/Regional) information on income, as well as information from local employers to estimate any general under or over estimation.

There is some evidence that questions on income in household surveys produce figures which are considerably less than income–data from other sources. This may be due to local variation as other sources on income do not provide data below county level. However, it may also be that people underestimate *household* incomes as only one individual responds or that interview surveys insufficiently well sampled produce a bias towards the unemployed, elderly, single–parent families as these are the households likely to be available during working hours. Thorough sampling is therefore crucial to ensure credibility.

A question on savings is also a pertinent one to ask in the context of housing and accessibility to the owner–occupied market in particular. Such questions are often avoided, as with income, and are more likely to get a response with an interviewer present to probe the interviewee.

4.4 Questionnaire Design

The design of the questionnaire is important in ensuring a good response rate for a postal questionnaire, less so for an interview based survey. The main points to consider are:

- **Length**
  Too long and it will put people off completing it, too short and it will not be worthwhile. A balance needs to be struck. A pilot study of the questionnaire can help iron out any problem areas as well as give some indication as to the suitability of the length.

- **Easy to read**
  It should not be cluttered and the questioning should follow a logical sequence; each question should indicate whether only one, or any number of options should be marked, or a blank space completed; little–known concepts such as shared ownership should be explained. This, once again, requires close liaison between consultant and client.

- **Credibility**
  A letter explaining why the council is undertaking the survey, emphasising the confidentiality of the survey and requesting the support of all the residents, to accompany the survey or form part of the questionnaire is recommended.

4.5 Sampling

4.5.1 Sample Size

When undertaking a district/borough wide survey, *there is no statistical basis for a 100% survey of the population.* A sample survey offers a means of obtaining information which is representative of the population as a whole, whilst saving on the costs that would be incurred by a 100% sample.

There is no threshold proportion of the population below which a sample becomes invalid. It is the total number of individuals sampled which is important, *not* the proportion of the overall population. With an increase in sample size, the reliability of the results improves. However, a point of diminishing returns is reached where there are no benefits in further increasing the size of the sample, and the additional cost would be wasted.

Deciding on the sample size for a survey depends on the intended use to which the informationwill be put. *The accuracy of the results increases little over 2000 cases.* When choosing the sample size, consideration needs to be given to the analysis of the results by sub–group and area which will be required. Unless the sample size is increased significantly, these results will be somewhat less reliable than for the sample as a whole.

Case Study
London Docklands

The Docklands Housing Needs Survey (1985) was based on a sample of 6,186 interviews from a population estimated at 221,000 households. *"As sample surveys go, this is a very large base – one household interviewed for every 36 households in the population. By comparison, some national opinion polls on people's voting intentions are base on samples as small as 1000, or one interview for every 41,000 voters. The large sample size decided upon for the DHNS was need in order to allow substantial analysis at single borough (and ward) level."*

4.5.2 Sample Frame

The most common form of sample is a random sample. The randomness minimises the effect of bias in the results and is achieved by giving all individuals within the total population an equal chance, theoretically, of being sampled. In order to obtain the sample, a sample frame is needed– a list of all the individuals or addresses of the households in the population to be sampled. A number of lists exist

- council tax registers
- electoral registers.
- small user file of the Postcode Address File (this is a list of delivery points which receive less than 20 items of mail daily)

None of these are perfect. However, registers of people such as the Electoral Register are more likely to be incomplete and to a greater degree than registers of addresses. It is a widely held belief that the electoral register is particularly incomplete with regard to the more mobile, and hence younger, and the disadvantaged in society, just the people who are likely to have a high incidence of housing need. However, where no other sample frame is available an electoral register can still be used with the results checked against other information eg. the Census, for inconsistencies or by using stratified random sampling.

A stratified random sample is a way of ensuring that certain groups of the population are adequately represented in a sample. For example, to enable analysis of detailed results for households in housing need, a higher proportion of households can be sampled in areas known to be more deprived. The 1991 Census Enumeration District information is useful in this regard. The results can be grossed up according to the proportions sampled in the different areas to reflect the population as a whole. (For more detailed statistical information see Marsh, C., *Exploring data: an introduction to data analysis for social scientists.* Polity Press, Cambridge 1988).

4.6 Choosing the Methodology – Postal or Interview?

The choice of whether to do a postal or interview–based survey is not always an easy one. There are some "rules of thumb" to help in deciding on the most appropriate methodology.

For a short, uncomplicated questionnaire a postal survey is more than adequate. The fewer questions requiring self–completion rather than a simple tick in a box, the better. When more detailed information is required, a face to face interview is obviously preferred as the interviewer can explain any ambiguity etc and can probe for further information (eg income)

A postal questionnaire for the same sample is obviously cheaper; conversely a larger sample can be interviewed for the same budget. When some breakdown of the information is required, for example, for districts in a rural area, a postal survey will give greater coverage and enable such analysis at this "sub–level" to take place. If the objective of the survey is only to obtain a district–wide picture, as in more urban districts, an interview–based survey may be preferred.

There is, essentially, a simple trade off between wider coverage, and hence more detailed analysis at sub–levels, and detailed questioning.

Interview surveys need to be carefully undertaken with regard to the sampling. Once the sample has been identified, interviewers will visit the chosen addresses to attempt to obtain an interview. Should the occupier of a sample address not be at home, good market research practice requires that the interviewer returns to the address up to four times, including evenings and weekends, to maximise the chances of interviewing the sample address.

If the occupier is still not available, the address is excluded from the sample and another, randomly selected address may be added instead. It is not sufficient to merely interview the next door neighbour who is at home and available. If sampling were done on this basis, it would not be representative of the population as a whole. It is likely that single person households would be under–represented and the unemployed and elderly would be over represented.

It is important therefore to question consultants about their sampling methods for both postal and interview surveys and the "re–call" policy on interview surveys.

4.7 Other Issues

There are a number of other aspects in the survey which need to be borne in mind whether organising a survey in–house or agreeing to commission external consultants.

- A pilot study is an invaluable way of ironing out any problems with the questionnaire, or the quality of the interviewers.

- If undertaking a postal survey, the mailing out of the survey is a major task and will comprise a significant proportion of the costs. For example the postage to send out 10 000 questionnaires, assuming a return rate of 50%, is £2,700! The envelopes, prepaid return envelopes and the actual "stuffing" of the envelopes all add to the costs. If much of the work is to be done in–house, this time consuming job is worth putting out to a private mailing company.

- The information gathered will need to be input onto a computer, which will be done as a matter of course by consultants. However if the survey is done in–house, authorities may not have the resources to do it themselves. Most universities have a data processing unit to process such information:

alternatively commercial organisations are able to undertake the data input.

- Primary analysis of the data requires particular computer software (usually SPSS) which some authorities may have in–house. However it is more than likely that this will be undertaken externally at an academic institution or by a commercial organisation. This will provide information of the frequency of responses to each question, eg 20% of population believe their homes are inadequate for their needs. More detailed "cross–tabulations" of the information such as adequacy of accommodation in relation to tenure or household type will normally need to be specifically requested.

- Secondary analysis of the data–this involves the analysis of the frequency tables and the specifically requested tables. Such surveys have the potential for providing vast amounts of data, some of which may not provide new or relevant information. Considerable thought needs to be given ahead of the primary analysis as to the combination for the cross tabulation to be requested.

If the Council has the computer capability to hold and undertake (primary) analysis of the data, the information can be made available to it on computer disc. If not, there is little point in requesting the data in such a format, a paper printout with all the frequency tables and requested cross tabulations will have to suffice. It may be possible to have further cross tabulations provided at a later date, but this is likely to incur further cost and is unlikely to be readily available.

4.8 Publicity

In order to ensure the maximum possible response there needs to be some publicity of the survey, and not just amongst council tenants. This can include:

- Preparation of a press release and contact with local newspapers to brief them on housing issues as well as the survey.

- Contact the local radio station who are likely to be interested in such a local issue, brief them on local housing issues and the survey. Suggest that the Director of Housing and/or Chair of Committee be interviewed.

- In rural areas it is important to contact parish councils to inform them of the survey and the reasons for it. This is particularly important where parishes have undertaken their own village surveys and may therefore think there is no need to complete another. Parish councillors can help to spread the word in their village about the importance of the survey.

- A poster informing people of the survey and asking them to complete their forms is another way of raising awareness of the survey. Such a poster should be placed in strategic places, eg post offices, public houses, village halls, community halls, town halls etc.

4.9 In–House v. Consultants

So, should the survey be done in–house or by consultants? What type of consultant? Firstly, whether the survey is carried out in–house or by consultants and whether it is the planning, social services or the housing department which is the lead department, a *lead–person* needs to be assigned to the task.

If the authority has a research department, or team within a department, with the relevant skills, some of the above work could be undertaken in–house eg. questionnaire design. Local authorities without this expertise are best advised to appoint consultants and to work closely with them. In practice, although some of the skills may be present in the authority, the major factor in deciding whether or not to engage consultants is the time–consuming nature of such a project (with work concentrated into a relatively short period).

By contrast to the detailed case studies (sections 4.2 – 4.5), East Hampshire District Council have undertaken a household survey (postal) in–house. The mailing out, collection and data input were contracted out, whilst questionnaire design and analysis of data was done in–house. The Council are to undertake a further district–wide survey on the same basis.

The in–house option has meant cost savings and closer contact with the analysis. The Housing Department, however, had to convince committee members and others of the objectivity of the data, in spite of the Council's close involvement.

Consideration also needs to be given to the expertise of the potential consultants. Local authorities should take into account both their proven ability to deliver the research aspect and a demonstration of their understanding of the housing and planning policies and strategy, to ensure appropriate analysis of the data.

4.10 Response Rates, Bias and "Grossing Up"

4.10.1 Response Rate

The rate of response, whether postal or interview survey will be significantly below 100%. The response rate for the London Household Survey 1986/87, an interview–based survey, is given below:

Total addressees issued	11,971	
minus ineligible addresses	1,654	
plus no. of households found multi–household address	464	
Possible interviews	10,781	(100%)
Refusals	2,648	
Non–contacts	2,107	
Questionnaires rejected at data processing stage	63	
Interviews achieved	5,963	(55%)

(London Research Centre)

Some postal surveys have obtained a response rate of around 50%, however a response rate of around 30% for postal surveys is not uncommon.

4.10.2 Bias

Data from surveys can be checked to ensure that there is no bias due to non–response. This can be done by comparing key variables eg. tenure with other data sources such as the Census or the Labour Force Survey.

It is a common occurrence in household surveys that there is a slight undercount of single–person households. This can be corrected by weighting the results for one person households. For example:

	LHS 1986/87	LRC Census projections 1986
1 person households as % of all households	30.0	33.3

The weight for 1 person households in the survey is 33.3 ÷ 30 = 1.11

In grossing up, the one person households will be multiplied by this figure as well as by the grossing up factor.

4.10.3 Grossing Up

The results obtained from a survey are for the sample surveyed, but as proportions represent the population as a whole. It may however be useful to know the number of households sharing amenities, for example. This requires what is known as "grossing up" to the population as a whole. For example, if the sample size is 1000 and the population is 100,000, the grossing up factor would be 100 000 ÷ 1000 = 100.

Care must be taken, for example, in "grossing up" the number of households in housing need in the district as a whole. As it is likely that those already, or likely to be, in housing need, will respond more readily to such a questionnaire, there is likely to be some bias towards these households in the response.

4.11 Funding

As the survey will provide information on the wider housing situation of the area, and not be aimed only at council tenants, there is a strong argument that a survey should be funded from the General Fund. In practice, joint funding between the HRA and General Fund is often agreed.

As the information gained is likely to be used by the planning department, part–funding from the planning department's budget may be negotiated. Where special needs/community care information is to be gathered, an element of the funding may come from the Social Services Department and the Health Authority.

Case Study
Llanelli Borough Council

Llanelli Borough Council (LBC) undertook a borough–wide housing need survey in the spring/summer of 1992. They approached a number of organisations who were known to the council staff as having experience in this field and invited them to prepare proposals for a borough–wide housing survey.

The objectives of the survey were to:

- estimate the need for additional and improved housing within the borough; give some idea of the fitness of the Borough's stock
- identify the aspirations, intentions and preferences of existing and potential households and the extent to which these could be met by the housing market
- assess the accuracy of the waiting list
- identify the nature and extent of demand for housing for people with special needs, including the impact of Care in the Community.

The consultants appointed were housing specialists, working in conjunction with a market research company who undertook the fieldwork. The survey involved personal interviews, by trained interviewers, using a structured questionnaire, on which the Council was consulted. The survey sample was 8,448 households representing 26.1% of the population and was stratified by ward, with 384 surveys carried out in each of the 22 wards. The consultants analysed then prepared reports on the results. The entire process, from commissioning of the consultants to receipt of the report, took six months.

Why did LBC decide to undertake a borough–wide housing need survey?

LBC believed that they required detailed information on all housing need in order to plan meaningfully for housing provision. Waiting lists provide only a partial picture of need, but the housing strategy must consider all need in the borough.

A consultant's report on various aspects of housing in the Borough, prepared in 1991, recommended a housing need survey reinforcing the Council's own view.

At a seminar organised with the Homelessness Forum (a group of local organisations including voluntary organisations, Probation Service etc) in February 1992, a number of the participants raised the need for a borough wide survey to obtain a more comprehensive picture.

The Welsh Office were encouraging local authorities to undertake assessments of housing need to provide a sound basis for formulation of plans. However, as there is no discretionary element in BCA's for Wales (see Chapter 2), LBC do not believe that undertaking the survey made any difference to their formula allocation in the last HSOP round.

Why did LBC decide to commission consultants to undertake the survey?

LBC considered undertaking the survey in–house. However, this would have required housing staff to devote two or three months entirely to the survey which would not have been feasible. They also considered employing students to assist with the fieldwork, supervised by LBC staff. This idea, too, was rejected as it was felt that such a survey warranted a professional undertaking.

Why was a personal interview methodology preferred to a postal one?

LBC officers felt that interviews offered a better chance of obtaining more accurate data, particularly given the complexity of the form which would have had to be shortened and simplified for a postal survey. If the cost for an interview survey on the scale carried out had exceeded LBC's budget, they would have had to consider a postal survey.

How was the survey funded?

Given that the survey was to assess all the housing needs in the district, the General Fund was considered the appropriate source of funding for the project. However, it was not possible to fund the survey from the General Fund alone, so the project was financed from both the Housing Revenue Account and the General Fund. LBC also considered the possibility of phasing the cost of the survey over two years, but this was not required.

The Housing Department had estimated the budget for the survey. It was fortuitous that the Chairman of the Housing Committee and other councillors were at the seminar mentioned above which was helpful in raising their awareness of the need for a survey.

Were any other organisations involved?

The Council sought the co–operation of Dyfed Social Services Department and East Dyfed Health Authority in assessing the requirement in terms of both the scale and type, of housing for people with special needs and for social housing for people who will be living in the Borough as a result of 'Care in the Community'.

How has LBC used the information obtained from the survey?

Principally to inform LBC's *housing strategy*. It confirmed the need for adaptations to existing stock and has encouraged the Council to consider very carefully the relative returns, given the limited resources available, from investment in existing stock compared to new build.

The survey itself, as was expected, did not give a definitive answer on stock condition as respondents were clearly not able to provide a technical view of the condition of their home.

LBC had hoped that the survey would indicate where the greatest need lay and where the best return for investment could be obtained. The analysis to date, although providing some pointers, has not provided the council with clear cut answers. This will require further analysis of the data available. The survey has however increased the Council's knowledge of the housing situation considerably and provided them with much relevant data. It provided information on affordability which has not been available before and the information on the intentions of people to move house, their tenure preferences and what they can afford is invaluable.

The Council believe they are able to address housing need in a far more logical manner than had been possible using waiting lists only and where cases were made on behalf of individuals irrespective of the wider housing picture. The survey also enables the Council to negotiate with confidence in presenting their case to the Welsh Office and housing associations.

The information has provided a superior base from which to guide *housing associations* and provide the strategic guidance sought by Tai Cymru.

LBC have used the results of the survey in their *bids for "top sliced" funding* eg. the Housing Market Package and the Flats over Shops initiative.

LBC are currently preparing a draft *Local Plan* which will be available for consultation at the beginning of 1994. In terms of affordable housing LBC are considering a policy which will seek to negotiate with developers for an element of affordable housing on sites of 2 hectares or larger. The information gained from the survey will be used to establish a target for the affordable housing to be provided in the borough, as a proportion of the overall number of houses to be developed.

In urban areas, it is unlikely that the evidence of need will be used at ward level in setting site specific targets, as such need could be met by a scheme irrespective of its location within the urban area. However, sites which are suitable for social housing will be identified in consultation with the housing department, giving regard to the categories of need and the location.

In the rural areas, where the exceptions policy is the only way in which affordable housing is likely to come forward (ie. the smaller villages), the ward information will provide a useful initial indicator of need in the village. LBC planning department would, however, require further detailed evidence of need in the village (see Chapter 5) as a pre–requisite for "exceptional" planning permission.

As a result of PPG3, which establishes a formal link between planning and affordable housing, and the guidance from the Welsh Office for housing departments to work in closer cooperation with their planning colleagues, there has been greater *co–ordination between the planning and housing departments* of LBC than had previously been the case. The Housing Needs Survey has helped cement inter–departmental relationships.

Making the most of the information

In LBC's experience, whilst providing a wealth of information on the housing situation in the area, the initial analysis of the data does not necessarily answer all the questions an authority may have. Considerable additional work is required either by the consultants or by the council itself. This will either add cost or require staff time and research expertise. According to Malcolm Boorer, Housing Manager of LBC, "the consultants report is only the beginning for local authorities".

LBC recommend that adequate time is given to deciding what information is required (ie which data to cross–tabulate) before embarking on more detailed analysis. This is particularly important when analysing at ward level, as in LBC's case, a cross–tabulation would need to be repeated 22 times.

Local authorities need to consider the computer software requirements for further in–house analysis of the data, as consultants will not hold the information forever. In LBC's case, for example, the information is available for 1 year. LBC have converted some of the data on to spreadsheets, using Supercalc, for in–house use. However, LBC point out that the information from a survey is rapidly out of date and use needs to be made of the data as early as possible.

Updating the information

LBC are considering how the survey data can be used to provide information on need over the longer term. They are considering further analysis of the survey data with regard to information on the adequacy of the council's waiting list for particular groups such as the elderly or families. Where there is a high level of correspondence between the two, this will enable some degree of monitoring of trends correlation through the waiting list.

How have other organisations used the information?

Private developers were not seen as a major audience for the results of the survey. Nevertheless one company approached LBC regarding the survey and are discusing a proposal which will include the provision of bungalows for which a particular need was revealed by the survey (both for rent and sale).

Dyfed County Council's (Draft) *Social Care Plan* for 1993/4 to 1995/6 includes a separate section on housing. In particular it refers to the findings of LBC's Housing Needs Survey with regard to special needs housing. These identified a very low level of demand for special forms of housing, but a high level of demand for support services and all types of adaptations to existing homes. The survey raised the awareness of the housing implications in implementing Care in the Community, and the particular needs to be met.

Local Housing associations were aware of the survey and the summary of results via a housing association liaison group. Associations currently developing in the borough were provided with more detailed information.

Case Study
New Forest District Council

In 1990 New Forest District Council (NFDC) undertook a district–wide housing need survey. A Housing Development Manager had recently been appointed who was given the task of assessing the housing need in the district as the Council realised that the waiting list did not accurately measure local housing need. The Council employed a part–time researcher with survey experience to undertake much of the work. The project was supervised by the Housing Development Manager.

The objective of undertaking the survey was to produce information which would help to:

- Target future homes to those parishes in greatest need
- Target future provision to the type of accommodation in greatest need
- Influence housing associations, developers and landowners
- Promote community involvement and support for appropriate development
- Plan bids for resources from Central Government and the Housing Corporation
- Justify the use of planning powers ie. local plans exceptions policies.

NFDC undertook a postal survey which involved sending questionnaires to 27.3% of the district's 65,630 households identified in the electoral register. In order to produce as accurate results as possible for all parishes, questionnaires were sent to 100% of the smallest parishes, 50% in the medium sized parishes and 10% in the largest parishes. In analysing the results, it was necessary to aggregate the data of some of the smaller parishes to produce statistically accurate results.

7,915 questionnaires were returned, which represented a response rate of 40%. An incentive of food hampers was offered to the first five completed questionnaires received. In addition, publicity for the survey involved contacting town and parish councils and issuing a press release, which led to the survey being mentioned in the local papers, and to a number of interviews on local radio stations.

Why did NFDC undertake a district wide housing need survey?

The waiting list was felt to be no longer an accurate indicator of housing need in the district. In addition, the council had not housed any households from the waiting list for a number of years and could therefore see little point in keeping one but some evidence of need to replace it was believed to be necessary.

There was a generally held perception that the New Forest, with an idyllic rural location, could not possibly have a housing problem. The Council wanted some hard evidence to dispel this perception. It was felt that a housing needs survey would help raise the awareness of the housing problem in the district amongst the general public, planning committee members and officers as well as the parish council and help to secure their commitment to meeting the need for affordable housing.

Although a number of parish surveys had been undertaken, this was only likely to be the case where the parish councils were in support of such an initiative and were concerned about the lack of affordable housing. Where parish councils were neutral or strongly opposed to any housing development in their village, the existence of housing need was unlikely to be revealed. A district wide survey would provide the council with a picture of need by parish, to support "exceptional" planning applications for affordable housing.

To achieve these objectives more detailed information was required than was available to the Council and a survey was seen as the best means of obtaining it.

Additionally the council wanted to be seen to be ahead of the field and thereby receive favourable treatment in terms of allocation of funds by the Housing Corporation and the Department of the Environment. The survey would also help to inform the HIP Strategy and meet the DoE's requirement that housing departments improve their knowledge of the local housing situation.

Why did NFDC undertake the survey in–house?

The main reasons for doing the survey in–house were the cost of consultants and the desire to keep close control of the job and ensure that the results would answer the questions posed. However, NFDC, had not appreciated the considerable amount of work involved in undertaking a survey and in analysing the data. It has been recognised that substantially more resources would need to be allocated to any future in–house survey.

Why did NFDC opt for a postal rather than a personal interview–based survey?

NFDC required information for each of its 36 parishes and an interview–based survey would have been too expensive to provide this coverage.

What was the extent of the involvement of other departments/organisations and what was the benefit of such involvement?

The planners were consulted on the survey from the outset, as the information obtained was to be of interest to them and because they had expertise in survey work. The Council's "Enabling Team", which involved every department in the Council, was consulted on the survey and kept informed of its progress. Housing associations, too, were invited to comment on the survey questionnaire and were kept up to date at regular liaison meetings.

It was felt to be important to involve all parties for whom the data from the survey would be of relevance, so that they endorsed the survey and felt a sense of ownership towards it. They would therefore be less likely to query the results if used, for example, as evidence of housing need to obtain exceptional planning permission.

NFDC also informed all the parish councils of the survey, its objectives and the information they were hoping to obtain and enquired as to whether the parish council would be willing to offer assistance in delivery. A number of parish councils assisted in this way which helped to raise the profile of the survey in that parish and allied the parish council to the Housing Department on the issue of housing need. In a number of cases where the parish council was involved, sites for affordable housing have been brought forward through the parish council which would otherwise have been unlikely to have been made available.

Given the objectives of the study, what were the salient questions asked?

- The occurrence of members of different generations sharing a bedroom and of brothers and sisters over the age of 10 sharing a bedroom to assess overcrowding.
- Concealed households requiring separate accommodation
- Respondents were asked what they felt they could afford to spend on housing, but there was no question regarding income
- People's perceptions of housing need, and the type of housing required.
- Some general information about the present accommodation was obtained, which enabled the accuracy of the survey to be checked against the Census.

How, and to whom, were the results of the survey publicised?

NFDC published a report on the results of their survey and a draft of their social housing strategy, which were available on request. They also organised a half day seminar to publicise the results and highlight the role of all the players in social housing delivery.

What use has been made of the information provided by the survey? What benefits have resulted from the undertaking of the survey?

The information has been extremely useful in identifying the location of *greatest need*, which is of particular importance in a district with many dispersed settlements. It has therefore been used to direct new development by housing associations, availability of sites and anti–development attitudes (NIMBYism) permitting.

NFDC produced a (Draft) *Social Housing Strategy* which assesses the need for social housing by parish using information from the Housing Need Survey on the number of homeless households, the waiting list for a given parish as well as the ability to solve the need through the existing social housing stock and programmed development. This assessment of need provides a clear indication of the number of properties required each year, the priority parishes for new social housing, the tenure split and the size of properties required.

Although the survey reveals that as many as 3,000 to 5,000 homes are required to meet the need for social housing which exists now or will arise over the next two years, NFDC acknowledge that the provision of homes on this scale is unrealistic. They have set their target as the elimination of the use of bed and breakfast accommodation and a limited amount of rehousing from the Waiting List.

The survey also reveals that there is a slightly greater need for shared ownership rather than rental housing. Nevertheless, the strategy gives priority to housing homeless households who generally have very low incomes. Shared ownership will be encouraged where this will meet an identified need and not divert resources away from rental housing.

Where the survey has been particularly useful is in targeting new housing developments to areas where the need is greatest. This, in fact, confirmed the Council's pre–survey concerns that these areas were being neglected by housing associations. In rural areas the survey has been used to inform the mix of social housing schemes. Such schemes have, as a result, included one bedroomed homes and bungalows rather than entirely family units.

The survey has been useful in raising the awareness of the housing problem in the district. Developers and other have offered sites for social housing as a result. Sites have been brought forward through the parish council, which may not have been made available had the survey not taken place.

It has been useful in demonstrating the good performance of the authority. NFDC was recognised by the Housing Corporation as the best enabling authority in the Corporation's West region and one of the top three in the Department of the Environment's South East Region. NFDC believes the survey has contributed to their high ranking. This good performance has paid off in terms of increased resources from the DoE in terms of both Basic Credit Approvals and Special (rural) Credit Approvals. The Housing Corporation, too, has made additional funding available to associations in the district. The Council believe that this favourable treatment can, at least partly, be attributed to having undertaken a survey. It therefore knows what is required and where; sites have come forward, the planners are on board, and money can therefore be spent efficiently and effectively.

The survey has provided evidence to justify the application for "exceptional" planning permission for social housing schemes. The planners have accepted this information as sufficient evidence of need, and do not require a further parish survey.

In terms of PPG3 and evidence of housing need to justify an affordable housing policy in the local plan, it has been useful in providing objective evidence of need. The survey also provides information on a local basis which could be used to justify site specific targets.

However, in terms of the numbers involved and the setting of a target for social housing sites on residential developments, the need identified in the survey exceeds the land available for *all* residential development. In addition to the need for affordable housing, the Council also needs to consider the demand for private housing whilst it is restricted by the restraint policies which prevail in the New Forest. The Council are therefore considering a target along the lines of the Housing Department's own strategy, ie the number of anticipated homeless acceptances each year. They are having to consider whether even this target is to be met via the land allocated in the local plan or whether additional "white" land will need to be allocated on which an element of affordable housing will be provided.

This possible flexibility and the planning department's embracing of the exceptions policy (4 schemes in 1991/2 and 4 in 1992/3) can be attributed, at least in part, to the survey which has made all involved give greater consideration to the need for social housing as it revealed considerably larger numbers than had been anticipated.

The survey has led to a wider awareness of the housing need in the district, throughout the Council. NFDC believe that it has been instrumental in bringing the housing and planning departments and committees closer together. In particular, since it was undertaken there have been regular joint committee meetings to discuss strategies and possible sites for social housing schemes.

Further use of the survey information and updates?

As the survey was, primarily, conducted in–house, the information is all held on the Council's computer. This required a considerable amount of time and staff input to ensure that the information could be held and analysed. However, the Council are not considering further analysis of the information as their priority now is to arrange sites for social housing schemes and ensure delivery of the homes.

The council's strategy for 1993/4 places more emphasis on housing homeless families, with some reference to the housing needs survey, but less than the previous year. The location aspect of the new–build strategy is that development should be targeted at the settlements where no new homes have been built in the last two years.

As such a survey provides only a snapshot of need, NFDC are aware that it should be repeated every three years or so. However, despite the fact that resource implications, both in the funding required and the staff time, make this difficult to realise, NFDC are currently considering an update.

The survey has proved to be more than worth the investment as it has attracted additional funds to the district and in terms of housing strategy information has provided data at a parish level. A further survey is being considered for 1994/95 to update the information and to provide data to justify affordable housing policies and the granting of exceptional planning permission for the lifetime of the local plan.

Case Study
London Borough of Hackney

Although the incidence of homelessness within the borough is seen by Hackney Council as the most concrete evidence of housing need– Hackney experiences one of the highest rates of homelessness in the country– the Council recognised the importance of considering the issue of access to homes in the borough. More information was needed on the relationship between local housing costs and incomes, particularly given that the average incomes in the borough are probably the lowest in London, but housing costs are about average for the capital.

In order to obtain data on access or affordability of housing in the borough and given housing authorities' strategic responsibility for monitoring housing needs, the Council commissioned a Housing Affordability Survey in summer 1992. The survey involved face–to–face interviews with 750 of the borough's 75,000 households. The primary aim of the survey was to relate housing costs to incomes, but it also collected data on housing circumstances and requirements.

The survey was carried out by a research company which was undertaking a London–wide survey but involving some 150 interviews in Hackney. A further 600 interviews were funded by LBH for which the questionnaire was somewhat amended (ie shortened) to suit their objectives and their resources.

Why did LBH undertake the survey?
Why was information on affordability so important?

LBH has been concerned about the inadequacy of funding available for the council to undertake capital works. HIP allocations are insufficient and the council has limited ability to generate capital receipts. The Department of the Environment is encouraging local authorities to raise resources by increasing rents ie. increasing the Revenue Contributions to Capital Outlay (RCCO).

LBH are against raising rents in principle, given the affordability problem in the borough. Nevertheless, they have had to increase rents by more than the DoE guidelines in order to fund the increase in planned maintenance. To strengthen their case to the DoE on the affordability problem, information on incomes in the borough was required.

Information on incomes from other sources was not considered adequate. The income data in the New Earnings Survey, which does have information by London Borough (and county), do not provide information on people who are not in employment, and are based on area of employment, not of residence. The Family Expenditure Survey only provides information for Inner and Outer London and not for the constituent boroughs. A household survey therefore needed to be undertaken to provide data on incomes of borough households

A further reason for Hackney undertaking a household survey was to obtain feedback on the views of council tenants on housing services and maintenance. Useful information could also be obtained of the profile of the council's tenants. For example, the council has no data on the type of households, and information on overcrowding and underoccupation from the Census was thought to be insufficiently accurate. A survey, with an interviewer to ensure uniform interpretation of questions, was seen to be far more reliable than self completion questionnaires.

An assessment of housing need was also recognised by the Borough as one of the criteria that the Department of the Environment are taking into consideration in their evaluation of local authority housing strategies.

How was the cost of the survey borne by the council?

The survey was funded jointly by the housing department, using funds from the Housing Revenue Account, and the Chief Executive's department (General Fund). The affordability information will be of use for the council as a whole. The housing information is not just concerned with council housing, but with all housing in the borough, thus justifying funding from the General Fund.

Why did the survey not include questions on, for example, the contribution of shared ownership to meeting housing need and people's aspirations regarding where they would like to live, preferred tenure etc?

For a representative response on shared ownership or for detailed analyses by tenure other than local authority rent to have been obtained, a far larger sample would have been required. The borough regrets not having been able to ask questions on people's preferences and satisfaction with their current accommodation, although such information would to a large extent have been hypothetical as the council is not in a position to do much to meet these aspirations. The small sample also prevents any analysis of deprivation in the private sector. However, the overriding reason for a shorter questionnaire was that the cost of undertaking a more detailed survey was beyond the council's budget and the information on incomes was of primary concern to the council.

The information from the survey could not be analysed at ward, or even at neighbourhood, level because of the limited size of the survey. At least a further 250 (1000 in total) interviews would have been required to enable sub–borough analyses to have been undertaken.

A problem with ethnic origin information and the sampling method

The wards to be surveyed were sampled at random and clusters of enumeration districts within those wards were selected which helped to keep costs down. Enumeration districts were therefore not random in the geographic sense. The result of this clustering was that, if a particular group of people was concentrated in a few enumeration districts, this group of people could be either over or under represented depending on whether their enumeration district was sampled or not. The Orthodox Jewish Community was under-represented in the Hackney survey as the sampling of enumeration districts was not truly random. This problem may however not be addressed simply by random sampling as wards to which such communities are located may not be selected in any case.

Why did LBH choose an interview based survey and why did they commission consultants rather than undertake the survey in–house?

Because the survey to be undertaken was wider ranging than merely gathering demographic data, as in the Census, LBH believed an interview survey was more appropriate. It was also felt that the interview methodology would provide more reliable information. The council did not have the staff resources available to undertake such a survey. In order to ensure the best quality work and data, the council believed that the best course of action was to commission consultants with considerable experience in the field.

LBH is also constrained regarding the amount of time that can be devoted to further analysis of the data which it recognizes will be considerably time consuming. The formal link to the research organisation which will be able to undertake analysis on request is invaluable to the council.

What use is LBH making of the survey?

The provisional results of the survey were used in the council's strategy document last year which was recognised by the Department of the Environment as being an important factor in embracing the enabling role. The information was also used in the council's Annual Report. The Borough's Unitary Development Plan has recently been on deposit . The information from the survey was used by LBH to support their affordable housing policy.

The council is to use the results of the survey, together with information from the Census and other information on need from research undertaken by the research section of the housing department, to inform its strategy for 1994/5. They are proposing to produce a separate detailed document on need to complement the strategy document. It will provide evidence for the council's case on affordability and therefore for more capital investment in housing.

The Council is also considering using the information on underoccupation to develop a database which will form the starting point for a more detailed survey on the type of housing, and its location, to which underoccupiers would consider moving.

Would the Council repeat the exercise?

As the council believes research and good quality information are vital for the council to carry out its tasks effectively, the undertaking of such a survey is seen as a worthwhile exercise, but LBH would have difficulty in justifying a repeat of the exercise in the foreseeable future. Although the Census provides useful data on housing need, the 10 year gap between censuses could justify a household survey to be undertaken toward the end of the decade. If the Government repeats the National Dwelling and Household Survey which it undertook in 1977/78, this could provide useful information on housing need, affordability etc. which could negate the need for a further household survey.

Case Study
Ryedale District Council

Ryedale District Council, a predominantly rural district in North Yorkshire, transferred its entire housing stock to Ryedale Housing Association in 1991. As it was no longer a provider or manager of housing, the Council could now focus its efforts on the enabling role. The large scale transfer of the stock realised a capital receipt of £7.2 million for capital investment in housing via Local Authority Housing Association Grant which the Council wanted to ensure was targeted at the greatest need. The Department of Environmental Health and Housing also realised there was a need for greater co–ordination of housing strategy and planning policies.

The Council recognised that in order to fulfil its strategic housing role successfully they needed to obtain a comprehensive picture of the housing situation in the district and the likely future housing need. They decided to commission a housing need survey. Given the limited staff resources within the Housing Department, the council invited a number of consultants to tender for the project. An interview was held with each consultant to discuss their proposal in more detail.

RDC appointed specialist housing consultants, who also had planning knowledge and experience, to undertake a housing need study which included a postal household survey. 100% of the smallest parishes (<200 population), 50% of the parishes with a population of between 200 and 1000 and 30% of the larger parishes and urban settlements were surveyed. The total sample size was 16,931, randomly sampled from the Electoral Register. This represents 43.7% of all households in the district.

The response rate was 49.7%, a total of 8,412 questionnaires being returned by the cut–off date. Given the size of some of the smaller parishes, the parishes/wards were amalgamated into 14 areas, for analysis purposes, to produce reliable data.

As it was a postal survey, the questionnaire contained no self–completion questions. There was however a space for respondents to make any comments about housing. Only 33 respondents criticised the survey and 18% of respondents made "additional comments".

> *"There are increasing problems with housing shortages for innumerable social/economic reasons and it is encouraging to see a*

District Council actually doing some research into the problem. I hope you do something practical with the information gleaned"
a respondent to Ryedale Housing Survey, September 1992.

Why did the Council opt for a postal, rather than an interview based, survey?

A range of survey methodologies was suggested by the various consultants who submitted proposals. These included a proposal to interview, face–to–face, 5% (1750) of the households in the district; a postal survey comprising 100% of households in larger areas and 40% of the smaller rural settlements; and the methodology outlined above.

The Council chose the latter, a postal survey, largely because of the rural nature of the district (over 100 parishes with a population of less than 1000). Information was required at sub–district level and if possible at parish level in the rural areas as a housing scheme in one parish would not necessarily be able to meet the need for other parishes. A 5% sample interview based survey would not allow any analyses at sub–district level.

What did the study brief include?

The brief required:

- demographic projections
- identification of those groups to which Ryedale's enabling role should best be directed
- forecasts and targets for new housing, including
    - housing groups
    - tenure
    - type of housing
    - affordability
    - distribution across the district
- proposals for phasing, performance indicators and review mechanisms

The consultants were to specify their own proposals for methodology and timescale. The Council had a set budget available for the study to which the consultants were asked to tailor their proposals.

Were any other departments/organisations involved in the commissioning of the study?

The study was commissioned by the Environmental Health and Housing Department. Other departments were involved, namely the planning department, the Council's solicitor and the Council's marketing team. Council Members were also involved in the commissioning of the study, the choice of consultants and comments on the draft report.

In the course of the study, the consultants contacted a number of other organisations to ascertain the availability of information on housing need (and supply) for various groups. These included:

- Housing associations and the Housing Corporation
- Housebuilders
- Rural Community Councils
- Rural Housing Trust
- Special Needs Housing Trust
- Social Services Departments
- Health authorities
- Voluntary organisations
- Local employers (present and future) including the Ministry of Defence
- Planning departments in both the District and County Council.

How important is the information on housing need to the planning department?

Given the realisation by the council of the need for greater co–ordination of the housing strategy and planning policies, the housing department and the consultants liaised closely with the district's planning department. The Council is currently preparing its district–wide local plan and information on the need for affordable housing was seen as crucial for the setting of a target for the proportion of housing which should be "affordable" and the formulation of an affordable housing policy which would seek to encourage developers to include affordable housing on residential sites.

The Council already has an "exceptions" planning policy and three schemes have been/are being developed on exceptions sites. The housing needs survey information provides information on where the greatest need is, which will enable the Council, and others, to target their efforts to these areas.

How was the survey publicised to the people of Ryedale District to maximise their response?

A letter was sent to all the parish councils in the district to inform them that the survey was to be undertaken and to enlist their support in publicising the survey. This was particularly important where a parish housing needs survey had been undertaken to avoid confusion between the local and district–wide surveys and to stress the importance of completing a further questionnaire.

The consultants produced a poster informing people about the survey and to encourage them to complete the form. This was placed at strategic sites by the housing department and Ryedale Housing Association. Copies of the survey were also sent to the parishes to be placed in post offices, village halls, public houses etc.

The local press were contacted and informed about the survey. Two of the local papers carried a story on housing in the district and the housing need survey in particular. The local radio station agreed to interview the Head of Housing and Environmental Health about the survey and the housing situation in the district on the morning that households were receiving their questionnaires.

A letter explaining why the Council was undertaking the survey and urging people to complete the questionnaire was included with the form. No incentive was offered for completion as it was thought that this would be difficult to implement without jeopardising people's perception of the confidentiality of the information they were providing.

What are the benefits from the information provided by the study?

The Council is now able to target funds available for LA HAG effectively as the survey provides them with a far more complete picture of housing need than was previously available.

It provides the Council with a basis for evaluating competing demands for capital expenditure in the district. RDC now has the information necessary to ensure that priority needs are met by housing associations when providing support for schemes requiring funding from the Housing Corporation.

It has established an information base against which both housing trends and the Council's performance as enablers can be judged. It also provides the information necessary to develop a comprehensive housing strategy statement.

The Council having undertaken the survey will be seen to be adopting a pro–active approach to its role as "enablers".

The Council now feel that they are able to negotiate with confidence to secure capital funding for housing need in Ryedale as the survey has provided them with an objective and comprehensive picture of the housing need in the District

The information on the survey also enables the planning department to formulate an affordable housing policy which can be supported at a public enquiry or an appeal by a developer

As a result of the survey and the broader study undertaken by the consultants, the Council has identified areas in which they need to do further work, in particular special needs and housing for the elderly and the enabling of affordable rural housing.

How has the information provided by the survey been made available to the public and other organisations involved in housing provision in the district?

As the survey report provided by the consultants is a detailed and lengthy report, the consultants prepared a short leaflet highlighting the main findings of the research which could be made as widely available as possible.

Chapter 5
Rural housing and housing needs surveys

5.1 Introduction

This chapter considers the particular reasons for housing needs surveys being undertaken in rural areas and looks at how various local authorities have become involved directly and indirectly. It is, arguably, in rural areas that housing needs surveys first became established as a means of assessing housing need.

5.2 The Rural Housing Crisis

In the early 1980's, waiting lists were becoming increasingly irrelevant as indicators of housing need in villages, where there was little, if any, chance of affordable housing being available. The right–to–buy, coupled with the absence of any replacement of social housing stock in these areas reduced the availability of social housing to nil in many villages. People therefore saw no point in applying to the local authority for housing and if they did, they were likely to state their preferred location as an urban area where there was more chance of housing being available.

As a consequence, the housing situation in rural areas was not perceived as being particularly problematic. Furthermore, housing associations, as the major providers of affordable housing, were in the main developing homes in urban areas where the evidence of housing need was more apparent.

To raise the awareness of politicians, both local and national, as well as the Housing Corporation, as the funder of social housing, parish councils, largely with the encouragement and/or assistance of the Rural Community Councils, began to undertake housing needs surveys, or include housing as a topic in village appraisals. These would provide them with evidence, and quantification, of housing need in their area.

In the late 1980s, a small number of local authorities were implementing, contrary to Government advice, "exceptions" policies and granting planning permission for low cost housing in villages where there was demonstrable housing need, and where they would not otherwise have allowed residential development. In 1989 the "exceptions" policy became acceptable. Indeed Government adopted it as recommended planning policy (see Chapter 2, section 2.2), and local authorities increasingly adopted exceptions policies. 75 local planning authorities had done so by 1991 according to DoE research (DoE 1991).

In order for affordable housing schemes on unallocated land in rural areas to obtain exceptional planning permission, planners require evidence of local housing need and a local housing needs survey has become the accepted means of providing this evidence.

5.3 Rural Housing Need Surveys

Such surveys are normally parish/settlement based and should, if possible, involve the local community. As the objective of these surveys is now to establish the scale and type of housing need, it is desirable, though not essential, that all the households in the parish are surveyed. The small size of rural settlements mitigates against sample surveys in any event (see Chapter 4, section 4.1).

Rural Survey questionnaires concentrate on the need for new housing and are therefore normally shorter than those for a district–wide survey where other information may be sought to inform the authority's housing strategy.

As well as providing evidence of housing need, necessary in prioritising schemes for funding, local housing need surveys are essentially an enabling tool in that they raise the local awareness of a housing problem, motivate individuals and agencies to bring forward sites and thereby assist in the delivery of affordable homes. There is an argument for local authorities, as part of their enabling role, to be more involved in the process than they may have been to date. This need not mean that local authorities will take over the detailed, "on–the–ground" work of others, such as rural community councils or parish councils, but they could adopt a strategic co–ordinating role and possibly some resources to support the fieldwork process.

5.4 The Options

A number of local authorities have addressed the process of assessing the need for housing in rural areas and a range of options are already in practice or have been piloted.

5.4.1 Rural Community Councils

A number of local authorities are working closely with Rural Community Councils who encourage, educate and assist parish councils on various aspects of affordable housing, including assessment of housing need and the undertaking of local housing need surveys. This often involves the local authority providing some funding for the preparation of the questionnaires and the analysis of the results by the RCC.

Case study
Cotswolds District Council and Gloucestershire RCC

Given the escalating rural property prices and increasing pressures for development in areas of restraint, combined with concerns for the future viability of smaller villages, Cotswold District Council recognised the requirement for a comprehensive appraisal, and a means of monitoring, of local housing need. In 1988, the Council commissioned a research project on the current and future needs of selected Cotswold villages. The research was also required to propose a means of developing a district–wide database on local housing need.

Following the recommendations of the research report (Gloucester College of Art and Technology, 1989) a partnership arrangement was set up between the Gloucestershire Rural Community Council (GRCC), Cotswold District

Council and the local parishes. A series of housing needs surveys have been conducted as a result of this partnership.

The process of undertaking a survey begins with an initial enquiry from a parish council. A fieldworker from the GRCC visits the parish council to discuss the issues of housing need and what a needs survey involves. The parish council receive a pro–forma survey form which can be amended to suit their circumstances. The final questionnaire is distributed by the parish council. The completed forms are returned in sealed envelopes to the District Council for input onto a personal computer, using the GLOSCAT village appraisal software package. The results are then analysed and a report is prepared which is sent to the parish council.

The village housing need survey reports include some information from the Census to compare and illustrate changes over time. National statistics are also included for comparison. The questionnaire includes general questions regarding the household such as current tenure; population profile; house type; length of residence; attitude to support for housing for local people; whether any member of the household has left the village and why; whether the household or a member of the household, is seeking alternative accommodation, etc. Questions are also asked about the accommodation required by households seeking housing, such as type of accommodation, what they can afford, whether they are on the council's waiting list, etc.

A follow up meeting is held after a survey is completed and the report distributed between the parish council, the GRCC and Cotswold District Council to discuss the next step.

The council has been operating this system since August 1991 and has undertaken 20 surveys (including a number currently being carried out) which help to build up a picture of housing needs in the district.

Cotswold District Council's planning department has produced a local plan working paper, "Affordable Housing and Planning", which forms the basis of the council's planning policy in respect of affordable housing and exceptions sites in particular. This document provides guidelines for an affordable housing policy in the local plan, placing emphasis on the identification of need via local housing need surveys.

> *"The plan will facilitate the provision of affordable housing on both "on plan" and "off plan" sites, where a local need for it can be demonstrated.*

"The plan will contain a policy setting out the criteria against which the proposals for affordable housing on "off plan" sites will be judged. That policy will make it clear that the proposal must be drawn up in the light of a local housing needs survey."

Housing need surveys are therefore a crucial element of the enabling role for this predominantly rural council.

ACRE, the representative body for Rural Community Councils, which has undertaken much project work on affordable housing in rural areas and has expertise 'in the field', provides training and advice to the RCC fieldworkers. It has also developed a computer software package to assist in analysing the data from local housing need surveys.

5.4.2 Working with Parish/Community Councils

In some areas where rural community councils do not exist, or do not take an active role in affordable housing, local authorities may work directly with the parish, or community council as they are known in Wales, to assess housing need in rural areas.

Case study
Preseli Pembrokeshire District Council

Preseli Pembrokeshire is involved in a programme of rural housing need surveys throughout the district. The impetus for these surveys dates back to 1989 when the council realised that housing for sale and rent on the open market was increasingly out of reach of local people, whilst the council's ability to house them was being steadily reduced. The council recognised that the provision of social housing required corporate commitment from all departments of the Council. A paper on social housing and the role of the planning system in facilitating the provision of affordable housing in rural areas on exceptions sites was presented to a Special Joint Meeting of the Planning and Housing and Environmental Committees.

"The first two steps toward a new initiative are a tight planning regime and to quantify the need.

"The release of additional land should be needs led and justified by accurate up–to–date local data provided...it will be necessary for each relevant community to be very closely involved in providing detailed local needs data to justify the release of additional land for low cost housing...The Housing Department can identify the areas which appear to provide the biggest level of unmet local need for further study."

The surveys are being undertaken in partnership with Community Councils who have agreed to deliver and recover the completed questionnaires on behalf of the District Council. The District Council prepares the questionnaires and analyses the completed responses. The questions included in the questionnaire are broadly the same as in the Cotswold's case study. The design of the questionnaire and the analysis of data is based on the software produced by the Local Jigsaw Campaign which is administered by the Geography Department of Aberystwyth University.

5.4.3 In Partnership with the Rural Housing Trust

The Rural Housing Trust, an organisation with considerable experience in affordable rural housing, has fieldworkers covering much of rural England. Part of their remit is to assess needs in villages with the parish council, where the latter has expressed an interest. These fieldworkers cover a number of districts each and liaise with, though act independently from, the local authority and possibly its housing strategy.

Case Study
Ashford Borough Council and the Rural Housing Trust

In addition to the Trust's regional fieldworkers, a unique appointment was made in Ashford Borough Council in Kent in 1989. ABC and the RHT jointly appointed, and continue to fund, a Rural Housing Initiatives Officer. Until this appointment, the planning department had been advising parish councils on affordable rural housing, housing need surveys etc., as well as having to determine planning permission for schemes coming forward as a result of this advice. The planning department were finding this dual role increasingly untenable and needed to divorce themselves from the role of parish council advisor. The appointment of the Rural Housing Initiatives Officer (RHIO) resolved this problem.

The main role of the RHIO is to liaise with parish councils and advise them on assessing housing need surveys and affordable housing in general. The Council solicitor initially wrote to all parishes about the RHIO appointment and those which expressed an interest were targeted for assistance. The parishes themselves have been involved in the distribution and collection of questionnaires with all households in the villages being surveyed. The results have been analysed by the RHIO.

Although Ashford (uniquely, and contrary to DoE Guidance) had identified sites for affordable housing in the local plan, planning permission for these sites, as with unidentified ones, is conditional on evidence of local need provided by the local housing need surveys. When a scheme is submitted to the planning department for outline planning permission, this survey information on housing need is sufficient, all other material considerations having been met, for the planners to grant outline planning permission and thereby give the go–ahead for the scheme to be worked up in more detail.

When detailed planning application is made, the planners require more definitive information on the actual households which are to be housed in the new development. A "second stage survey" may be undertaken by a housing association or by the RHIO. This normally involves a letter being delivered to every dwelling in the village informing them about the scheme and asking them to apply if they are in housing need, providing details of the household, the type of housing needed and their income. Such second stage surveys not only provide information on the households to be housed, but are also a means of updating the original survey which may have been undertaken two years ago. The local need is likely to have changed during this period.

The "second stage survey" may also be undertaken via an advertisement in the local paper, asking people to apply, or via a public meeting publicised to the local community at which application forms are provided. Alternatively, households interested in housing to be developed could be asked, in the initial survey, to identify themselves.

The Ashford experience has been that the "second stage survey" reveals a need for a half or even a third of that identified in the initial survey. However, when the houses are being built and people see that there is a real chance of being housed, more people come forward who are in housing need in the village.

As a result of this partnership, seven affordable rural housing schemes were started in the first year. Ten more are currently being developed and bids were made to the Housing Corporation for funding for a further 13 schemes in the 1993/94 allocation round. The council and the trust agree that the success of the scheme is largely due to the independence, from the planning department in particular, of the Initiatives Officer. Some of the parish councils are wary of the district council and are far happier providing information on housing need to an independent individual as they were concerned that the housing would genuinely house local people in need rather than people from the council's waiting list who would not have a local connection.

The Council view their funding of the work of the Rural Housing Initiatives Officer, of which the assessment of need is a major element, as part of their enabling role.

5.4.5 Rural Housing Enablers

ACRE has recently piloted a model for increasing the provision of affordable housing in rural areas by the private sector, including housing associations, of which the assessment of need has proved to play a major part.

Case Study
The ACRE Model

The model was recommended in a report commissioned by ACRE (Clark and Dunmore 1990) which involved a sequence of stages for the development of a social housing scheme and the appointment of a Rural Housing Enabler who would activate and orchestrate these stages. The model was piloted in five authorities across the country where the Rural Housing Enabler (RHE) was appointed by ACRE working through the Rural Community Council, but independent of all agencies (ACRE, 1993).

The initial stage of the model is the establishment of local need. This involved the RHE's working closely with the parish councils to carry out housing needs surveys, including designing the questionnaire and advising parish councils on the logistics of carrying out a survey. There was some degree of apathy in some areas on behalf of the parish councils to become involved. This is one of the problems of a needs led approach to social housing provision as housing will only be provided where there is a parish council willing to get involved in undertaking a survey. A village with an urgent need is likely to be ignored in the provision of housing, if the parish council does not show an interest in the first instance in being involved in a housing need survey.

One survey was not generally regarded as having sufficient evidence of need as those expressing an interest in social housing in an initial survey did not come forward on the same scale when schemes were completed. A second stage survey to assess the actual rather than the potential need was deemed necessary.

These second stage surveys took on a variety of forms. In one authority a second stage survey form was designed by the RHE. The forms were placed in a public place in the village and individuals were invited to complete them and return them to the RHE who registered any firm needs on the District Waiting List. In another district, those people who had identified themselves in the initial survey as being in need were asked to put their names on a list which was then passed on to the housing association developing the scheme. Another option is to establish a register of need with details of the rent levels etc, clarifying that it is not a "waiting" list.

Housing need surveys not only provided a means of establishing the need for social housing in a given parish, but were also useful in opening up channels for educating the parish council about housing. They helped to build up the confidence of the parish and to establish a rapport between the parish and the RHE which is vital if the delivery of affordable housing is to be successful.

Parish councils and other agencies involved in social housing thought that a RHE who was independent of the council had advantages. The RHE acts as an "honest broker" between the parish councils and the District Council, which is of particular comfort to the parish councils who are concerned that the housing developed provides homes for local people.

5.4.5 District–wide Housing Needs Surveys

The assessment of rural housing needs may also be addressed in a district wide housing needs survey, as in New Forest District (see section 4.3), where this is accepted as providing sufficient information to inform the council's housing strategy, support for housing association schemes and for applications for "exceptional" planning permission. No second stage survey is required under this approach.

Chapter 6
Assessment Of The Need For Supported Housing

6.1 Introduction

In formulating comprehensive housing strategies, and to assist the implementation of Community Care, local authorities must now address the need for supported housing, as well as housing for people with other special needs (eg single homeless; wheelchair housing) as detailed in Chapter 2. Preparation of a strategy or Community/Social Care Plan will require local authorities to have an awareness of the type and scale of need which also provides a basis for making a case for additional capital and revenue resources (Cook, S.,1993). This Chapter considers how the need for supported housing may be assessed.

6.2 Housing Need Surveys

Surveys of the type discussed in Chapter 4, can provide some information about the number of people with disabilities and the requirement for some form of supported or mobility/wheelchair housing.

Case Study
London Borough of Camden

A housing need survey commissioned by the Housing Department of the London Borough of Camden in 1992 included a section on health, disability and special needs. The survey (undertaken by face–to–face interview) revealed that 16,000 households (19%) have an adult or child with a disability. The majority of those with a disability had either a chronic illness/sickness (44%) or experienced mobility problems (30%). 7% were wheelchair users with a further 1% requiring a wheelchair. Almost half found the use of stairs to be a problem.

The Council related the number of wheelchair users to the number of wheel chair accessible dwellings within the local authority and housing association stock. The mismatch between need and supply was found to be a shortage of 620 suitable units.

Case Study
Christchurch Borough Council

One of the objectives of the housing need survey commissioned by Christchurch Borough Council and Twynham Housing Association was to assess the extent and nature of demand for housing for people with special needs and the need for housing for people "returning" to the borough as a result of Care in the Community.

Given the high proportion of elderly residents in the borough, the survey included questions on physical disability and the need for adaptations to the home as well as the need for a variety of support services.

The survey revealed that 13% of all households had one or more persons with a disability or illness which makes climbing stairs difficult and that 1% of households included a person who is a wheelchair user. 2% of households identified some adaptation, most commonly stair lifts and rails to baths and showers, which would make coping in their home easier.

Only 18 households, or 0.55% of those surveyed, expected a member of their family to return from some kind of long term hospital or institution in the next 5 years. Further inquiry was made about their likely accommodation requirements eg. returning home; households moving to accommodate a person returning; setting up home independently and setting up own home but with some kind of support.

Where questions might require follow up from a voluntary or statutory organisation, such as for care support requirements or adaptations, respondents were asked to provide their names and addresses which were passed on to the appropriate organisation for action.

A question on special needs housing requirements is relatively complex. Although arguably better suited to a face–to–face interview than to a postal survey, the information relating to housing need likely to be provided by surveys will be fairly general, giving little more than an indication of the probable scale of households with a member who has a disability.

The relatively small numbers of people requiring such housing, can mean that the information obtained is not representative of the population as a whole, particularly not at a local, or parish level. Information on closure of long stay hospitals, for example, and the consequent housing need created, will not be addressed by these *household* surveys. In order to obtain a more complete picture on the need for supported housing, local authorities might consider some complementary means of assessing this aspect of housing need.

6.3 Imbalance in Existing Provision

The joint DoE/DoH circular (1992) on Housing and Community Care suggests that housing authorities draw up a picture of housing *supply* and need in the area and identify cost–effective and practical objectives. With some notable exceptions, the supply of supported housing to date has in general been somewhat ad hoc with various agencies and local organisations involved in its provision. As a result housing authorities are unlikely to have a complete picture of the supported housing stock that exists within their area.

The first logical step for assessing the need for supported housing would be to investigate the full extent of supported housing both in its own area, and in neighbouring districts as some homes may cater for a wider geographic area. This process will provide some indication of the groups for whom there is an obvious undersupply, eg people with a learning disability, mental health problems, frail elderly etc.

Case Study
Housing Care and Supportin the New Forest District (2)

The housing department in New Forest District Council had established a special needs housing forum which was unanimous in its concern that the Council was not addressing the need for supported housing. The Council sought to establish the supply of supported housing currently available in the district, but a complete picture could not be provided.

The Council commissioned a consultant to undertake a study to assess the supply of supported housing in the district and to indicate what the priorities should be for future development of supported housing.

The study identified three possible sources to meet future need for supported housing, namely new housing association schemes, local authority and housing association relets and existing properties no longer needed for their traditional purposes. It included a review of the available funding for supported and other special needs housing and the proportion of Housing Corporation rented programme for Hampshire which was devoted to special needs in previous years.

A complete audit of the existing stock of supported housing was undertaken, which included information on client groups, housing type, length of stay and funding source. Further analysis of the likely sources of housing demand was carried out, including long stay hospital closures, existing households, short stay accommodation, vulnerable single homeless, residential schools and children's homes, and family placement where it is used as a short term solution.

This information enabled the consultant to assess the priorities for future developments and recommend a number of schemes and assisted the Council in making a strong case for capital investment in supported housing.

The Council has found this study to be extremely useful. The Housing Corporation is now stipulating that around 15% of its programme will be targeted towards special needs housing allocated on a county by county basis. Social Services tend to have a county–wide view and do not consider the likely housing need by district. New Forest District Council is now able to make the situation in its area known to both the Housing Corporation and the County Council.

This ability is particularly important at present as it would appear that the Housing Corporation's allocation policy for the special needs quota is based on who can make the strongest case. Housing Corporation Policy Statements have stated that where a case can be demonstrated for special needs, a scheme to meet this need is more likely to receive funding than one where no evidence of need is provided.

6.4 Special Needs Housing Forums

A number of authorities have set up special needs housing forums which are normally made up of representatives from the housing department, housing associations in the district, the Social Services Department, Health Authority, Probation Services, and local voluntary sector organisations (MIND, Abbeyfield Society, Mencap etc). These forums can prove most useful in identifying the range of supported housing need and in assessing the current supply and likely future demand for particular types of housing. Local voluntary groups and housing associations often have a well developed local knowledge of special needs.

Endorsement of priorities for funding by these bodies can prove difficult. There was little agreement in the New Forest example amongst the diverse groups represented on the forum. Each representative, not unreasonably, pushed for housing to be developed which would best meet the need of the particular interest group they represented. Decisions have usually been based on the relative merits of different scheme proposals rather than on a fundamental assessment of the need for supported housing or of an imbalance in supply (Watson and Harker, IoH/NFHA, 1993). An objective, independent study such as the one commissioned by New Forest provides the local authority, as the strategic housing authority, with the information necessary to make an informed and rational appraisal of the priority schemes for funding.

Membership of a Special Needs Housing Forum is essential for all organisations involved in the provision or management of special needs or supported housing to ensure that the needs of all groups are considered.

As part of Community Care planning, County Accommodation Groups are being established (eg. Hampshire, Suffolk) to ensure that housing is not overlooked in the Community/Social Care Plans. The assessment of the need for supported housing in individual districts undertaken, or commissioned, by Special Needs Housing Forums is vital in order to ensure that the County Accommodation Group consider needs which may differ between districts.

Unitary local authorities, pre– and post– local government review, are arguably better placed for Community Care Planning as housing and social services departments will be part of a single authority and therefore will not have to compete with needs in other districts for funding for priority schemes. However Special Needs Housing Forums will remain important vehicles for assessing the type, scale and severity of need for which supported housing is required.

6.5 Special Needs Registers

Local authority waiting lists to date have rarely enquired about special needs of applicants in terms of purpose–built dwellings, necessary adaptations or care requirements. As a result, the majority of people with special needs do not bother to register on Council waiting lists as they believe there is little opportunity of being housed in suitable accommodation.

Swale Borough Council discovered this to be the case with special needs groups interviewed by the Council's Housing Project Officer who was endeavouring to ascertain the requirement for special needs housing locally. The group representing people with physical disabilities believed that social housing organisations were not providing suitably adapted properties and therefore saw little point in registering on a waiting list.

A number of councils are looking at ways to assess not only the scale of need for particular groups but also the particular needs of individuals as these can differ considerably. One option being considered by a number of authorities in Kent (Gillingham, Rochester and Swale) is the establishment of a special needs register. Another is to include a section on special needs in the housing waiting list application form.

Case Study
St Edmundsbury Borough Council – Special Needs Register

St Edmundsbury Borough Council has been concerned that insufficient information is available on the housing needs of people with physical or mental disabilities:

> *"It is quite clear from my experience that, whilst Health and Social Services have a wealth of information on their clients, it is understandably both care and health related, and it does not address the housing issue" (Stephen Cook, Chief Housing Officer, St Edmundsbury Borough Council)*

The future demand for supported housing needs to be assessed. In particular, those people who are currently living with parents, who provide care without assistance from the statutory agencies, are likely to have a housing (as well as a care) need when their parents are no longer able to care for them.

In order to obtain a better idea of the need for supported housing, St Edmundsbury together with all the district councils in Suffolk, believe the way forward is to enable Community Care (ie supported) housing needs to be identified as part of district councils' housing registers. The districts and the county in Suffolk have agreed a common list of questions which will be incorporated in each district housing application form. This will provide the client based information at a district level.

The special needs assessment section of the waiting list is to include questions on individuals' disability, mobility, the type of housing and amount of support they require/are likely to require and when it will be required. Applicants are also asked where they would like to live.

The intention is to provide the information in a standard format to the County Housing Policy Officer so that the needs are identified at both the county and district levels in the Community Care Plan. The information on need will also enable the districts to make a strong case for funding for special needs housing to the Housing Corporation ADP.

> *"Until we can clearly demonstrate need, there is no hope of bringing in additional resources, either capital or revenue."*

In order to ensure that those people who may be in need of special needs housing come forward to register, local authorities have to publicise the changes to the waiting list which have taken into consideration the needs of people with disabilities. There remains the recurring waiting list dilemma that if people do not see any hope of being housed appropriately, they may not believe it worthwhile to apply. Evidence of a commitment, particularly by actually developing a scheme, will encourage people to come forward and register as they will feel there is a greater chance of being appropriately rehoused.

Another way to help to publicise the special needs register, and overcome reluctance to do so, is to establish good links with voluntary organisations and to persuade them and Social Services to encourage their clients to register their need or likely future need. A Special Needs Housing Forum provides an excellent vehicle for informing the relevant organisations of the existence of a register and for eliciting their support and assistance.

Publicity for a special needs register also needs to be undertaken to raise awareness of people who may currently be managing without assistance but who may require care and/or suitable housing at a later date.

Given the overall shortage of funding and in particular the limit on revenue funding in the form of SNMA (Special Needs Management Allowance, SNAP in Scotland), Social Services and Health Authorities need to consider the implication for community care housing. Consideration should be given to the possibility of top slicing the transfer money which they are receiving from the Department of Social Services. The assessment of need is, once again, crucial in establishing now much transfer money is needed. The ability to justify the requirement for funding will depend on the identification of need.

6.6 National Studies; Local Application?

A number of surveys and studies have been undertaken at the national level to assess the prevalence of disability amongst the population as a whole and the likely need for housing for people with special requirements.

6.6.1 The OPCS Disability Survey (1988)

The OPCS Disability Survey revealed that 6.2 million people (14.2% of the population of Great Britain) had some form of disability. As it was a national survey, based on a sample of 100,000, application of the figures at sub–national level poses problems of accuracy and reliability. The survey did not enquire specifically into the housing requirements of people with disabilities.

In the absence of other information on disabilities it can provide some guidance on the potential scale of the problem and the likelihood of particular housing requirements amongst the elderly in particular. The survey provides data on the proportion of the elderly population with disabilities and the number with severe disabilities. The information is further broken down to provide data on the type of care and support required.

Case Study
Survey Of Special Housing Needs in Bath And Wansdyke

A survey of the need for special needs housing in the city of Bath and in Wansdyke District estimated amongst other special needs requirements, the need for sheltered housing for the elderly using the OPCS Surveys of Disabilities in Great Britain. The proportions in the national survey of people requiring different degrees of care and support were applied to the elderly populations of Bath and Wansdyke. Where the severity of need is such that assistance is required at some time of day or night (categories 1–6 in the Survey) for those elderly people who live alone, the study assumed that sheltered housing was required.

This assumption together with a further assumption about a proportion of elderly people who prefer not to go out, but are not housebound and for whom sheltered housing would provide a sense of security, provided a gross figure for sheltered housing need in 1992 for the area. The figures were then compared with the existing provision in the area to arrive at the net need for additional sheltered housing.

The survey also made use of the information in the national study on the adaptations thought to be required by disabled people and their carers. The latter gives some useful indication of the likely scale of adaptations which will be required in a district for elderly disabled people which can be used to inform bids e.g. for Disabled Facilities Grants and Minor Works Grants.

Estimated number of people aged 60 or over in Bath requiring adaptions to their homes

Kind of Adaption	Proportion nationally of people with a personal care disability: % with each adaption	Proportion nationally of people with a personal care disability: % wanting further adaptions	total % needing adaptions	Number requiring further adaptions in Bath: 1991	Number requiring further adaptions in Bath: 2001
Ramp outside	5	4.2	9.2	110	120
Hand rail outside	8	4.6	12.6	120	130
Ramp inside	1	0.8	1.8	20	20
Hand rail inside	22	8.4	30.4	220	240
Door altered – better access	2	1.3	3.3	30	40
Stair lift	1	6.7	7.7	180	190
Other alterations – better access	1	0.4	1.4	10	10
Fitted furniture altered	2	1.7	3.7	50	50
New bathroom or toilet added	3	7.1	10.1	190	210
Shower installed	10	18.9	28.9	500	550
Door answering/opening system	1	3.4	4.4	90	100
Any adaptions	38	42	42	1110	1220
All aged 60 or over with personal care disability				**2650**	**2880**

6.6.2

A report, *The assessment of the housing requirements of people with special needs over the next decade (NFHA 1992)*, has been produced by the National Federation of Housing Associations together with the Office for Public

Management. This study uses secondary data sources, both published and unpublished, which have been made available by independent and voluntary agencies representing people in the different groups to produce estimates of housing need among particular groups. Those primarily considered are people with learning difficulties, and mental health problems and the frail elderly.

The study concentrates on the impact of demographic economic or policy changes which are likely to affect the demand for special needs housing in the future, such as the closure of beds in long–stay institutions.

The report suggests that the model used to assess national requirements for special needs housing can be replicated at local level, which is thought to be a more manageable task than at national level. In developing a housing strategy, local authorities will need to consult with other agencies in relation to special needs groups. The report provides some useful data sources and details the factors influencing the need for additional housing for people with special needs.

Data Sources for Assessment of Housing Requirements for people with special needs

Issues	Sources of Data
Hospital closure plan	District and Regional Health Authorities
Demographic trends	Planning department, OPCS
Changes in admission to residential homes	Social services departments
Surveys of existing user needs	Housing authorities, social services departments, housing associations, voluntary agencies
Estimates of future needs and special needs for certain groups	Social services departments, voluntary sector agencies, self help groups and housing associations

Source: NFHA/OPM (1992)

Factors influencing the need for additional housing for people with special needs

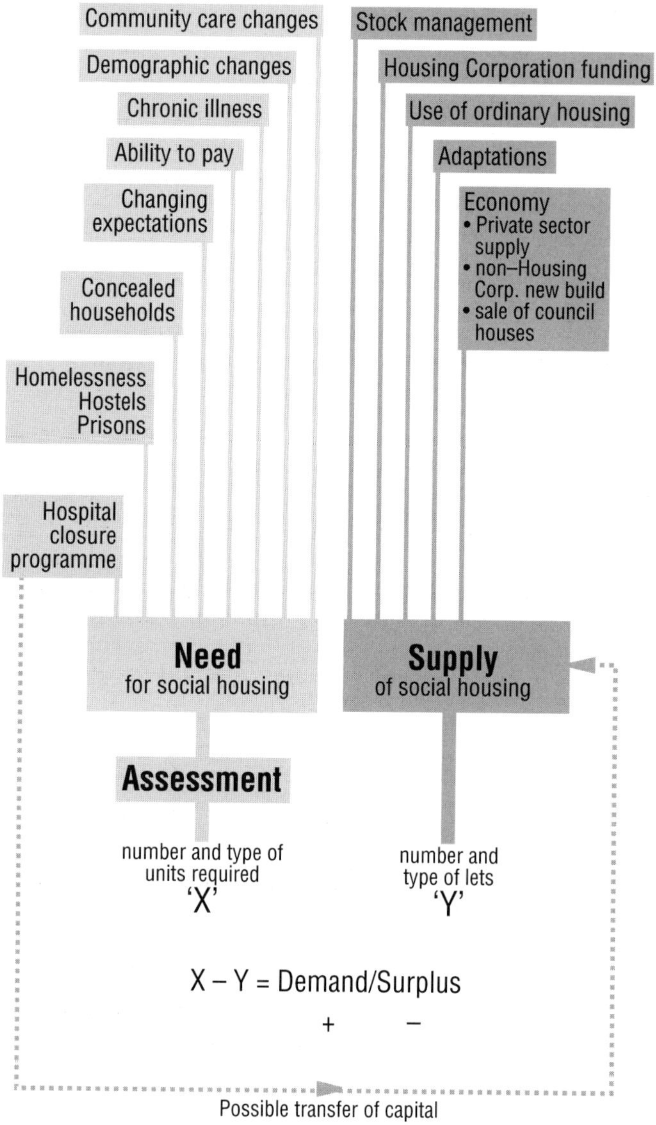

Source: NFHA/OPM (1992)

6.6.3

A further study – *Community Care Planning: A Model for Housing Need Assessment* (Watson and Harker, 1993) – recently published by the Institute of Housing and the National Federation of Housing Associations considers one particular client group, people with learning disabilities, and proposes a "moves and shifts" model for assessing their additional housing needs. This model is inspired by the "gross flow" approach of Whitehead and Kleinman used in their review of housing needs assessments for the Housing Corporation (Whitehead and Kleinman 1992) which links the movement of households and the supply of homes in different tenures and divides households up into different groups. It also takes into account the possibility of mismatch between need and supply.

The "moves and shifts" model for special needs housing, which produces a five year forecast for the need for supported housing in the social rented sector, also separates the sources of demand for housing according to the current range of living circumstances among the population concerned (eg. people with learning disabilities). It attempts a more comprehensive and systematic approach to assessing housing need than other methods considered in this chapter as it is based on analysis of people's living circumstances and the factors triggering moves between different types of accommodation. A simplified version of the model's procedure is shown below.

The "Moves and Shifts" or "Housing Pathways" Model

1. Divide population into groups by living circumstance – eg. family home, hospital, shared housing etc)
2. Apply housing need factors to each group – eg. family stress, discharges, poor tenancy/self catering wanted/tenancy break down from local survey evidence, care management recording systems, published data on demographic and accommodation trends

Continued over

3. Calculate housing need figure for each sub–group

4. Sum the housing need figure for all the sub groups

5. Subtract housing supply factors: re–lets, programmed new–build, private sector solutions, moves within existing provision

6. Add mismatch of need to supply

Stages 1 – 6 produce Net Housing Need

(Watson/Harker, IoH/NFHA, 1993)

The model has been used to provide a national estimate of unmet housing need for people with learning difficulties. The authors are of the view that a suitably adapted model could equally be used for other needs groups. They also suggest that the model will work best in an area which is large enough to contain a range of different forms of accommodation and small enough to produce reasonably accurate figures for people living in different circumstances, ie an area with about 100,000—150,000 population for people with learning disabilities.

The model is felt to be most sensitive at local level as the assumptions made are likely to be most realistic at this level, given the detailed knowledge of the population and local resources. The model provides a basic framework which will need to be tested out in local areas and amended according to local circumstances.

It is worth noting that the model requires information on the supply of special needs housing in the area, which may call for a special audit of existing and programmed new–build.

6.7 Studies of Particular Groups

In order to obtain detailed information about the specific housing needs of a particular group in society, a study dedicated to investigating the needs of this group might be undertaken.

For example, the housing needs of single people are particularly difficult to identify. Firstly, single person male households are the least likely group to complete and return questionnaires, as has been shown in the 1991 Census. Local authorities have no statutory responsibility to house single people and therefore may not accept single people on their waiting lists. If they do, they often stipulate an age limit, usually of 25 and above. As registering on a waiting list holds less hope for single people of being rehoused, waiting lists are likely to be even less representative of single people in housing need than of other groups. People living rough, a high proportion of whom are single people, are not sampled in a household survey. Whilst an audit of rough sleepers was included in the 1991 Census, it is widely recognised to be significantly lower than the true figure.

Local authorities may therefore consider undertaking a study of the needs of single people to obtain information on the housing needs and aspirations of this group which it would not be able to obtain from existing sources. A number of local authorities have already done so eg. Guildford, Harrogate and Reading Borough Councils.

Case Study
The Housing Needs of Single People in Harrogate

Harrogate Borough Council commissioned a study on the present and future housing needs of single people in the Borough. The objectives of the study were to:

- examine the extent and nature of housing needs of single people
- examine the extent and quality of current housing provision,
- investigate the possible options for meeting single persons housing needs
- develop an action programme.

The researchers' methodology involved both quantitative and qualitative methods including analysis of existing information on need and provision to the Housing Department, relevant voluntary agencies, local housing associations, Probation Services and Social Services. Other sources of information were the housing needs surveys carried out by parish councils and the survey of houses in multiple occupation undertaken by the Department of the Environment.

To forecast future need, use was made of the OPCS population projections including information on migration and age profiles and the DoE's figures on the rate of household formation. Discussions were also held with the planning department.

A series of interviews was undertaken with "front–line" workers in the local authority, voluntary and private sectors in order to assess the types of housing required by single people. In addition, the study included interviews with a sample of single people in various categories of housing need in order to ascertain the type of housing needed and the particular problems experienced in trying to secure appropriate accommodation. Potential interviewees were identified in co–operation with advice and referral agencies.

The study was unable to quantify the precise numbers of single people in housing need in Harrogate Borough. Nevertheless there were significant numbers of single people seeking advice from HBC's Aid and Advice Centre. In addition, agencies dealing with "special needs" had considerable number of clients in housing need. Compared with the supply of housing for single people, there was clearly a need for additional housing for single people. As single person households were an increasing proportion of the population, this was likely to be reflected in the numbers of single people in housing need.

Based on the information collected the researchers made several recommendations to the Borough regarding the housing needs of single people, some of which the Borough have implemented. These include giving priority to affordable housing schemes for single people and the borough working with housing associations to develop partnership schemes for single people and encouraging associations with experience of managing and developing special needs housing for particular groups into the Borough.

In addition the borough is endeavouring to increase the contribution of the private rented sector eg through working with the Civic Trust to extend the "living over the shop" scheme. Single people throughout the borough are being encouraged to register and obtain advice from the Housing Aid Centre. The Borough has set up a single person's working group, partly as a response to the Children Act. HBC is represented on Partnership Groups for Community Care Planning, which will involve increasing co–operation on single persons housing requirements.

In addition, the Council is considering, as a result of the result of the study, the redesignation of a proportion of its current stock of elderly person's housing for use by single people.

A study on a particular group can therefore provide detailed information, both quantitative and qualitative, on the housing needs of that group. Care should be taken, however, to ensure that the needs of the group which has been the subject of such a study do not overshadow other equally pressing needs which are not addressed by the study.

6.8 Qualitative Research of Particular Groups

Qualitative studies undertaken regarding the well–being and care requirements of, for example, the mentally ill or the physically disabled, can provide some useful information on the types of accommodation required, eg supported housing, adaptations etc. However, these do not provide any valid indication of the *scale* of housing need. The housing requirements of those individuals interviewed cannot be taken as representative of the entire population as the sampling of these surveys is more incidental, ie by word of mouth, rather than with a statistical sampling base.

Chapter 7
The Planning System and the Assessment of Need for Affordable Housing

7.1 Introduction

The importance of the assessment of need in implementing "exceptional" planning policies for low cost housing for local people in rural areas has been discussed in Chapter 5. This Chapter considers the assessment of need for the formulation and implementation of planning policies, following PPG3, to secure an element of affordable housing on residential sites.

The requirement of evidence of need to support these policies has been established in Chapter 2. Consideration now needs to be given as to what will constitute acceptable evidence to Inspectors at Local Plan Inquiries and whether that evidence is sufficiently robust to withstand appeals by developers.

At the time of writing, few local authorities had completed the whole process of needs assessment, local plan preparation and local plan inquiry, and no examples of appeals by developers against evidence of need had been reported. No precedent has therefore been set. This Chapter aims to provide some guidance for local authorities in assessing housing need to provide evidence for affordable housing policies and considers DoE guidance and the experience of some local authorities.

7.2 Department of the Environment Guidance

The starting point for any affordable housing policy in the development plan is a survey of the housing needs of the area over the plan period, according to the DoE's Draft Explanatory Note on Planning and Affordable Housing. Unlike Scottish Homes, which has commissioned best practice guidance, neither the DoE nor the Housing Corporation for England have decided to provide any national criteria, or guidance for assessing local needs, for either rural or urban affordable housing policies. "*There is no single recipe*" for such surveys, according to the Draft Explanatory Note, which refers authorities to the Audit Commission report on the preparation of local authority housing strategies.

The word "survey" in the DoE Explanatory Note is misleading in this regard. It does not imply that the Department is in fact providing some guidance on methodology in suggesting that local authorities undertake household surveys as detailed in Chapter 4. What is meant by "survey" is some form of assessment of need. This may be based on information already available to the local authority, eg waiting lists, Census information, homelessness figures. It could also involve a household survey, particularly where existing information did not provide a complete picture of housing need. Where the local authority sets a target for social housing which could be vulnerable to challenge, a survey could provide robust evidence to support it.

Although there is little guidance on the type of assessment which will be acceptable some idea of the information which will be required is provided. Assessments of housing need should take account of:

- local market conditions eg. house prices and rents
- the size and needs of households
- what households can afford
- availability of financial resources.

In setting targets for affordable housing for the district as a whole, and for specific sites, local authorities must be realistic in terms of the available funding for social housing. They are also required to plan balanced communities and 100% affordable housing on residential sites would be unacceptable, even if the need identified indicated that all available land for residential development would need to be developed for social housing.

> "*It will normally be desirable in planning terms that new housing development on a substantial scale in both urban and rural areas*

should incorporate a reasonable mix and balance of house types and sizes to cater for a range of housing needs."

7.3 Robust Evidence of Need

Whether the evidence to support an affordable housing policy in a local plan is sufficient, is a matter for the Planning Inspector to decide. It is not possible to anticipate what individual Inspectors will consider acceptable evidence of housing need, however local authorities which have undertaken household surveys, or comprehensive studies, will be in a stronger position than those who have not done so.

The local authority must feel confident that the information it has provided to justify an affordable housing policy will withstand cross–examination.

Cambridge City Council, in considering the scope of the evidence required on housing need to support an affordable housing policy at public inquiry obtained Counsel's opinion on the matter. Robert Carnwarth, Q.C. is of the opinion that the following evidence pertaining to housing need and supply will be necessary:

- Detailed evidence of housing need in Cambridge both at present and projected into the future
- Evidence which defines "affordability" in the Cambridge context
- An evaluation of the need for "affordable" housing (as defined).
- Identification of the potential sources of "affordable" housing over the Local Plan period
- An evaluation of the extent to which such housing must be provided on allocated housing sites.
- Evidence as to how "affordable" housing may be made available at realistic values on allocated sites in private ownership

Case Study
Housing Need in Cambridge

In the light of the serious affordability problem in Cambridge, the City Council is looking to the private sector to contribute to meeting housing needs. They therefore needed to establish what the actual level of need for affordable housing would be in such a way that would withstand cross–examination at a Local Plan Inquiry and commissioned a study which had the following objectives:

- to justify policies in the Local Plan which seek affordable housing
- to give weight to negotiations for affordable housing
- to justify refusals of planning permission on specific sites where applicants have been unwilling to negotiate/include affordable housing.

The study would therefore meet the detailed requirements contained in the Counsel's opinion, which had been obtained. The major elements of the study were to forecast the need for affordable housing (1991–2006) and the estimates of the number of different types of affordable housing required (social rented, equity share and bottom of the market owner occupied housing).

The "Gross Flows" Model

The Property Research Unit of the Land Economy Department at Cambridge University were commissioned to undertake the study. They assessed the likely scale of additional housing using a model which has been developed over the past 10 years, and was the method used by the Department of the Environment to produce a medium term forecast of housing need in 1977 – the last time an official Government estimate of national housing needs was undertaken. The methodology, known as the "gross flows" model, was used recently in the work undertaken by the researchers for the Housing Corporation, to assess the need for housing at a national level.

The "gross flows" approach takes into account the movements of households into and out of the housing system and the propensity for various groups to choose owner occupation, as well as inter–tenure moves.

The demand for affordable housing includes that from newly forming households who choose not to enter owner occupation, moves from the private rented sector and owner–occupation and demand from migrants. Part of this need can be met from the private rented sector and part by local authority and housing association relets. The remainder provides the estimate of housing need in the city using demographic sources.

Estimates for concealed households, replacement of unfit stock and existing backlog of need are added to the demographic figure to obtain the overall figure of additional housing needed. The components of the model and the basis for determining the scale of additional social housing units required are shown below:

The "Gross Flows" Model

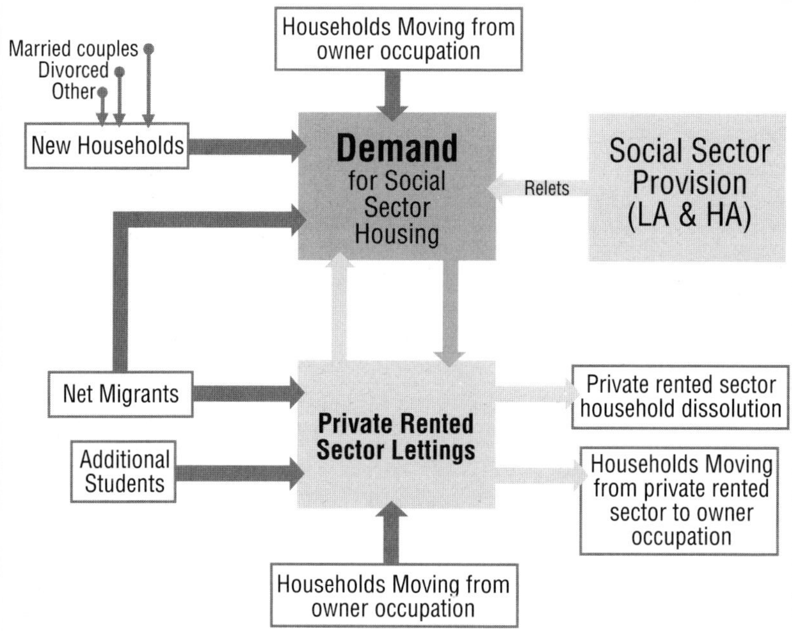

Sensitivity Analysis

The model enables sensitivity analysis to be undertaken, altering the assumptions on which the model was based such as the future level of relets, the tenure preferences of households and the growth in student numbers

Information Sources

Where possible, local data sources such as the 1991 Census are used.

Where information is only available at a county, regional or national level these figures are appropriately scaled for Cambridge, eg the Labour Force Survey which provides information on national propensities for different tenures.

In some specific areas, such as estimating the scale of concealment and for local information on the extent of movement between tenures, data from local household surveys would prove invaluable in improving the accuracy of the model.

Affordability

In assessing local housing needs, some analysis of the local housing market and local incomes is suggested as being a useful indicator. This approach does not model directly the relationship between incomes and house prices. Whether a household is able to afford owner occupation is dealt with indirectly through the modelling of the tenure propensities of new households, determined by demographic factors and past trends. As such it deals with long run trends in housing need, rather than assessing affordability or access problems at a particular point in time, which the authors argue are extremely sensitive to house price volatility.

Cambridge Factor

The study focussed on issues of significance to the Cambridge housing market. These include the impact of students and a possible new settlement outside the city.

Supply

The study also involved some analysis of the supply side of social housing and the resources likely to be available to meet housing need. The projections of need and supply are compared to derive estimates of the future shortfall. A target for the proportion of residential development which will comprise affordable housing is derived from the number of additional homes required and private sector output. This, however, does not include the projected housing association developments which will increasingly have to compete with private sector projects for land on the open market.

Such a rigourous approach provides a means of assessing the likely housing need over the 10 or 15 year period covered by the Local Plan and Structure Plan review. This is an important factor in setting targets and justifying affordable housing policies which will apply for the lifetime of the plan, or until review.

Whilst the model provides a robust methodology for assessing needs over the relatively long term, it does not provide information on the size of accommodation required, or on people's aspirations and preferences, such as where they would prefer to live. It also provides no indication, for example, of the contribution shared ownership might make in meeting housing need, as it is based on past trends which do not include shared ownership as a separate tenure, and does not consider information on household incomes, necessary to assess whether shared ownership is feasible. Nor does it provide information on special needs housing.

The authors of the study, themselves, bemoan the lack of local information and state that local household surveys could provide this information. Such a study undertaken in conjunction with a sample household survey, could provide the housing and planning departments with the information necessary to prepare and implement housing strategies and formulate and implement affordable housing policies which are valid for the plan period.

Cambridge City Council are to use the information provided by this study to support the inclusion of an affordable housing policy in their local plan and to set an overall target for the proportion of residential development which will be affordable housing.

7.4 Waiting Lists

In contrast to Cambridge's comprehensive study into housing need and supply and the net–projected need for affordable housing over the life time of the local plan, another local authority has merely used the waiting list as the evidence of need.

As the number of households registered on the waiting list represented 50% of the Structure Plan requirement for the number of dwellings in the district, the authority has set its target for affordable housing at 50% of residential development. No account is taken of local authority and housing association relets or of the accuracy of the waiting list as an indicator of need. Any changes over time are also ignored. This evidence, in spite of a clear need for affordable housing, will be difficult to defend on cross–examination or appeal.

7.5 Use of available data

Other local authorities have provided evidence based on a rigourous analysis of existing information available to the authority, and undertaken the work in–house.

Case Study
Southern Derby Local Plan Inquiry

In the Southern Derby Local Plan Inquiry, July 1992, the Inspector requested information to support the Council's affordable housing policy. The Housing Department submitted evidence on the:

- Council's waiting list,
- operation of the points system,
- increase in applications for housing
- increase in "homeless" households seeking accommodation
- figures illustrating its inability to house applicants from the waiting list.

According to the Council, forecasts of need and supply, based on the increase in homeless families and the total supply of lettings, indicate that it is unlikely to be able to house all the homeless households within the next two years.

The evidence also made reference to the study on access to housing by Glen Bramley (1991) which reveals that access to owner occupation is limited for newly forming households under the age of 30 in Derby. 45.5% of these households can only afford to rent.

Based on the evidence submitted, the Inspector concluded that the problems of housing in Derby remain acute and will worsen and that the need for affordable housing provision in new developments is very compelling.

> *"The need for further affordable housing provision Derby is clear–cut. The detailed evidence of the Council on this matter is both convincing and of immediate concern to me... In a nutshell, I find it to be substantial and urgent"*.

The Inspector is convinced by the evidence available to the Council that the need for housing is such that the maximum, yet reasonable, use should be made of affordable planning policies to contribute towards a solution to the problem. The local authority does not set a target for the area as a whole, but sets targets for the proportion of affordable housing to be provided on particular sites.

Evidence of need was not required to justify the targets set for each site. Indeed, on one site the Inspector recommended that the Council should increase the affordable housing target, or state that it should be the *minimum* number of affordable homes provided on the site. This was not based on evidence of need relating to that particular site, but on the overall need for affordable housing in the city.

Although some information on house prices and incomes of waiting list applications was provided, it did not provide a complete picture of affordability in the city. However, the Inspector in this case did not require analysis of this type.

This is the response of one Planning Inspector to a particular Local Plan. It by no means sets a precedent for future local plan inquiries. However, it does provide some insight into what might be required in practice, although this is likely to depend on the Inspector designated for the Inquiry as well as the demand from other objectors for more detailed evidence of need.

7.6 Defining Housing Need

Local authorities in setting a target for the proportion of housing in the local plan which is to be affordable must be realistic in defining housing need, both in terms of what constitutes need and in particular the demand for *additional* housing, as well as in setting the contribution required from new–build.

In formulating a housing strategy, the local housing authority will consider the requirements of existing tenants when assessing housing need eg. households without central heating might be "in need". This would not require additional building. The local plan, by contrast, is primarily concerned with *new* development. This has to be taken into account in preparing the evidence to support an affordable housing policy. Households requiring adaptations should not be included in the overall figure for *additional* affordable housing.

Where an assessment reveals a need for a certain number of homes, analysis will need to be undertaken as to what element of this it will be met by:

- the open market, ie what proportion can afford to purchase a suitable home without subsidy support
- relets, both local authority and housing association
- conversions and rehabilitation
- flats over shops, and other initiatives

Where the contribution of any of these methods in meeting need is limited or negligible, local authorities should illustrate that this is the case. Failure to do so is likely to raise objections to the authorities evidence of local need and supply in the Local Plan.

Care must also be taken when considering waiting lists as evidence of need where they include requests for transfer. Meeting these requests will result in an existing dwelling becoming available and must be taken into account to avoid double counting. However, given the likely mismatch between accommodation vacated and required, some additional housing may be necessary.

7.7 Affordability

In both PPG3 and the subsequent draft explanatory note, the Department of the Environment emphasise the need for information on houses prices and wage rates in the area which will provide some guidance as to what constitutes affordable housing.

In addition, the Planning Division of the DoE includes open market housing at the lower end of the market as "affordable" housing.

Some analysis of affordability is therefore necessary to justify "seeking to negotiate" an element of affordable housing on residential developments and in setting targets for provision. This will also assist in identifying what constitutes "affordable" open market housing and the contribution this will make to meeting need. Some guidance on sources of information is given below.

> *"Such policies should give clear guidance on what the authority would regard as affordable housing in this context (taking account of the economics of housing provision in the area)" PPG3, para. 38*

7.7.1 House prices

The Halifax and Nationwide Building Societies are the major sources of information on house prices.

The *Halifax* provides information quarterly on a national and regional basis. Information at sub–county level is available on request. Data is available by house type, which is useful as an average house price conceals the price of homes at the lower end of the market which first time buyers and others in housing need may be able to afford.

The *Nationwide Building Society* also produces quarterly reports on house prices on a national and regional basis. Data is also available at sub–county level on request.

The information provided by these building societies at a district level may not include sufficient transactions for each type of house to be representative of the local market. It can be supplemented or replaced by information obtained from *local estate agents* and other advertisements for houses and flats for sale (or sold) in the area. This will provide information on the local housing market by size/type of dwelling and by sub–area if necessary.

The annual *New Earnings Survey* by the Department of Employment provides information on incomes at the national, regional and county level. If this information is used as a proxy for income levels at district level, any local differences in incomes will be obscured. Moreover it relates to people who work in an area rather than the people who live there, and does not derive information on non–earners or income from sources other than employment.

7.7.2 Incomes

Much of the information on income is not available at district level.

The Family Expenditure Survey is possibly the best source of available data on income. It is produced by the Central Statistical Office with information at regional level. However, because it shows how income relates to factors such as tenure, occupation and household composition, it is possible to draw some conclusions about the likely level of income in a particular area.

A household survey is therefore invaluable, as it gives income data at the district or borough level.

Case Study
London Borough Of Hammersmith And Fulham

The London Borough of Hammersmith and Fulham's Research and Information Services Group undertook some research on the affordability of house purchase (and private rent) in the borough. This research provided supporting evidence for an affordable housing policy in their Unitary Development Plan. The tables below illustrate the affordability problem in the Borough.

Minimum Household Incomes Required to Buy Housing at Lowest Decile Prices in Hammersmith and Fulham

	Property Price	1989 Minimum Household Income Required	Property Price	1991 Minimum Household Income Required
1BR	£62,000	£19,630	£55,000	£17,420
2BR	£80,900	£25,620	£70,000	£22,170
3BR	£95,600	£30,270	£85,200	£26,980

Source: Hammersmith and Fulham (1992)

Gross Household Income Distribution for Hammersmith and Fulham 1992

Income Bands (£ per annum)	Owner Occupiers %	LA/HA Renters %	Private Renters %	Total %
£0–3,899	9	33	14	19
£3,900–7,799	7	36	15	20
£7,800–10,399	4	10	3	6
£10,400–15,599	11	9	15	11
£15,600–18,199	6	4	9	6
£18,200–20,799	7	2	3	4
£20,800–25,999	11	3	5	6
£26,000+	45	3	35	27
Total	100	100	100	100
Non–response rate	17	10	15	14

Note: Percentages may not always add up to 100 due to rounding.
Source: Hammersmith and Fulham 1992

The income data used is from the London Household Survey 1992. LBHF contributed additional funds to the survey to enable an increased sample of households in the Borough to be interviewed.

The tables show that very few of the households who are currently renting would be able to afford to purchase a home. The London Survey enabled further analyses of this issue to be undertaken. Interviewees were asked whether, given the choice, they would prefer to buy their own home. Of the one or two person households who would prefer to purchase a home, only 3% of public renters and 37% of private renters could afford the cheapest one bedroomed accommodation.

On the basis that this more recent research indicated that whilst the affordability problem has eased, approximately 60% of households still cannot afford market housing in the Borough, the target for affordable housing has been reduced from 80–90% to 60% of all new development.

In terms of the realities of funding this amount of affordable housing, Proof of Evidence from the Borough Environment Department, for the Public Local Inquiry stated that the Housing Corporation Funding likely to be available in the borough over the next three years, some £65 million, would be sufficient to enable 60% of all new housing to be affordable.

The Inspector's response is awaited.

7.8 The Affordability Gap

Further sources of information on affordability are the studies commissioned by the Association of District Councils and the House Builders Federation, undertaken by Glen Bramley, which provide a means of assessing the extent to which new, younger households in particular areas may be able to afford different housing options.

These reports proved most useful in their estimates of the national need for social housing of around 100,000 new homes per annum. At local level they are more useful in assessing the proportion of new households who can afford owner occupation and shared ownership and the proportion who can only afford social rented accommodation, than they are at estimating the actual need for additional housing. This model considers new households under 30 years of age only, thus any figures of need given will be underestimates of the total need.

Any study of affordability based on house prices and incomes at a given time can do no more than provide a snapshot not a forecast. Studies of this type need to be updated as house prices and mortgage–to–income ratios change.

Case Study
East Cambridgeshire District Council:
Housing Needs And Affordability

The Affordability Gap model has been adapted for use within a single district. East Cambridgeshire District Council wanted to assess the feasibility and implications of producing a methodology to assess housing need and commissioned a research project to adapt the SAUS Affordability model to the district. The model is linked to demographic projections and information on the supply of housing to forecast the number of new homes required to meet the housing need of new households, broken down by household size and tenure. It is also capable of testing the impact of changed conditions.

The study provides figures on the ability of households in the district to purchase suitable accommodation, as in the national studies (see table below).

The district model also provides estimates of the proportion of new households able to buy a suitable property for five sub areas. The number of new households in each area requiring social housing over a five year period was also calculated, and compared to the number of relets likely to be available to obtain the number of additional social housing units required.

Sensitivity tests were applied, such as lower house prices and lower levels of relets for younger households, which resulted in the affordable housing proportion of overall development varying quite considerably. However, the need for affordable housing remains a substantial part of total provision (between 17% and 42% district wide)

A different version of the model could be developed to analyse the extent of housing needs among older households. This would require a more complex model which would need to include indicators of wealth and dependency.

Ability of New Households to Purchase a Home

Area	ADC/HBF Affordability Studies				East Cambs Model	
% of new house-holds able to buy	1989		1990		1991	
	new 1BR	new 3BR	new	2nd	new	2nd
East Cambs	39	11	23	47	35	49
Cambridge City	38	10	16	30		
Fenland	32	7	25	47		
Hunting-don	42	16	15	29		
Peterborough	36	15	23	41		
South Cambs	44	7	26	47		
East Anglia	50	8	27	49	46	58
South East	50	13	19	48		
England	54	21	24	45	34	50

Source: Bramley and Lambert (1991)

East Cambridgeshire District Council have also commissioned a household survey which will provide information on:

- incomes, as well as savings and assets,
- what people are willing to spend on different housing options;
- people's aspirations and preferences of tenure, type and location of housing;
- concealed households and households inadequately housed.

The model is to be updated with the information from this household survey, together with information from the 1991 Census which will enable the accuracy of the affordability model to be enhanced.

The District Council, which has recently transferred its stock to a housing association, recognises the importance of its strategic and enabling roles. The information from the affordability study, and the household survey, will underpin the Council's housing strategy for the future. The ability of the model to forecast future need is particularly useful as local housing authorities are now required by the Department of the Environment to prepare strategies over a three year period.

It is intended that the final version of the model will be made available to the council. This will enable them to update the model over time as variables change, eg house prices

The Council is also particularly concerned that the usable capital receipts, resulting from the voluntary transfer of its stock, which are to be invested in housing, are targeted to meet the most urgent housing need. The study will enable the Council to identify where housing is most needed and what types are required.

The information from the affordability study has been made available to the Council's planners as they prepare the Local Plan. The initial results of the study were incorporated in the Supplementary Planning Guidance of the Local Plan. In addition, the Council's intentions regarding further research into affordable housing were made known to the inspector at the Local Plan Enquiry in 1992.

The Council's affordable housing policy seeks to encourage developers to include an appropriate percentage of affordable housing in new residential development on larger sites (20 units). The Supplementary Planning Guidance will give further information on the district–wide target for affordable housing, based on the affordability study and household survey.

There were few objections to this policy, which the Inspector has recommended should remain unchanged. One can assume that the evidence of need for affordable housing provided by the studies commissioned by the Council have convinced the Inspector that the affordable housing policy is justified.

7.9 Targets

PPG3 and the Draft Explanatory Note both refer to local authorities setting targets (not quotas) for the proportion of new residential development in the local authority area which will constitute affordable housing. Local authorities are also able to set targets for specific sites taking site and market conditions into consideration.

Whereas for rural exceptions sites, evidence of local need is required for each scheme, in urban areas it is more difficult to define "local" need. Therefore using evidence of local need to set targets for urban sites may not be possible. An affordable housing scheme in an urban area will meet need arising from the urban area as a whole and not just the environs adjacent to the site. It therefore follows that evidence of overall need in an urban area is sufficient, and is not necessary at a more local level.

7.10 Long–Term Needs Assessments

The assessment of housing need in the area should cover the future development plan period (DoE, December 1992). Housing strategies also now need to cover a three year period. Housing need surveys, however, only provide information of the housing need at a given point in time. Some information can be obtained from surveys on the likely need for housing over the next three, or possibly, five years, but the response to questions regarding the need for housing beyond that should be treated with caution. The information becomes increasingly unreliable as the period of projection increases.

Where information on housing need over the long term is required, studies such as the "gross flows" approach or the "affordability model" (as detailed above) provide the most sophisticated methods currently available of forecasting need.

Some calibration of waiting lists and other on–going information, set against the data from a household survey, might also be possible.

Information on household and population projections also provide some long term indicators on housing need (see Chapter 8). These have been used with the "affordability model" to produce forecasts of housing need.

Chapter 8
Secondary Sources of Information on Housing Need

8.1 Introduction

Existing information on population growth and from national surveys can help to obtain a picture of existing and future housing needs. This chapter looks briefly at the major data sources and the information they provide on housing which is of relevance to the preparation of housing strategies.

8.2 Population Estimates and Projections

Each year the Office of Population Censuses and Surveys (OPCS) produces estimates of the population in England and Wales by single years of age and sex. The estimates for local authorities and health authorities are grouped into five–year age groups. National estimates are also produced by legal marital status.

Monitor PP1 92/1 Provisional mid 1991 population estimates for England and Wales

Series VS no 18 PP1 no. 14. Key population and vital statistics:local and health authority area. (This volume also contains local birth, death and migration statistics)

Projections of the national population have been produced since 1919. They are produced by the Government Actuary's Department and are now produced in alternate years. The most recent set of national projections is based on the mid–1991 population estimates.

Monitor PP2 93/1 Population projections:Mid 1991–based

Series PP2 no.17 Population projections 1989–2029

(Series PP2 no. 18 Population projections 1991–2031 is due out summer 1993)

Sub–national projections are produced for the larger authorities in England i.e London Boroughs, metropolitan districts and counties, as well as for regional and district health authorities. These projections are made in close collaboration with the Department of the Environment. Similar sub–national projections for authorities in Wales and Scotland are made by the Welsh Office and the General Register for Scotland respectively.

OPCS Monitor PP3 Mid 1989–based population projection for local authority areas in England

OPCS Monitor PP3 Mid 1989–based population projections for health authorities is England

Provisional mid 1991–based short term population projections (1992–1994) are available from the OPCS offices. The final mid 1991–based figures are due out in September.

Series PP3 no.8 Population projections; area; 1989–2015

1989 Based Population Projections for the Counties of Wales, Welsh Office (1991)

Population Projections (districts and regions): Scotland (1989 Based). Registrar General, Scotland 1991

The sub–national projections may not take full account of local authorities development plans which, if successfully implemented, could modify current demographic patterns on which these projections are based. (For a detailed explanation of the methodology used to produce these sub–national projections see Armitage (1985): *Population Projections for English Local Authority Areas,Population Trends, No. 43, HMSO.)*

An illustration of the housing implications of demographic data is shown below for Ryedale District Council.

Ryedale District Age Structure Projections 1981–2006

Age	Base year 1981	End 1986	End 1991	End 1996	End 2001	End 2006
0–14	11680	16918	17666	18729	19642	19612
15–29	18200	19654	19587	17368	16866	17448
30–44	17700	18961	19280	20584	21146	20919
45–retirement	17400	18139	19458	21626	22650	23276
retirement+	15500	16854	17953	18925	19856	21206

Source: DCA (1992)

The number of people over retirement age in Ryedale District increases very significantly by nearly 2000 between 1991 and 2001. Within that group the number of people over the age of 75 is projected to increase by nearly 1100 by the year 2002 of which nearly 600 are over the age of 85. Note also the decline in the number of people in the 15–29 cohort which further emphasises the picture of an ageing population profile in the District in the years to come. This demographic data which illustrates an ageing population has clear implications for the housing strategy, in particular the need to address a growing requirement for housing for the frail elderly.

8.3 Household Projections

The Department of the Environment publishes projections of *household* numbers at national, regional and county level (as well as metropolitan districts and London Boroughs) based on the population projections and headship rates.

Department of the Environment 1989 based estimates of Numbers of Households in England, the Regions, Counties, Metropolitan Districts and London Boroughs 1989–2011, published by the Government Statistical Service

Similar household projections are also produced by the Welsh Office and the Scottish Office.

In addition, the planning departments of county and regional councils and unitary and Island authorities prepare there own population and household projections. Local authority housing departments should therefore consult the planning departments in their own authority as well as the county planning department, where relevant, for demographic information.

A number of external organisations also produce population and household projection. The ones mentioned most often by local authorities are The Chelmer Institute (Anglia Higher Education College) which has developed the Chelmer Model, and the London Research Centre.

8.4 The 1991 Census

The Census was carried out on 21 April 1991 and provides considerable information at ward and enumeration district level relating to households which can be used in assessing housing need. The Census is unique because it provides almost 100% coverage on a consistent basis throughout the country. Some degree of continuity of statistics over time enables comparisons to be made between censuses. Comparisons of housing needs and circumstances can be made within and between local authority areas.

List of Topics in the 1991 Census (England and Wales)

Household Topics	**Person Topics**
name [1]	sex
address of enumeration [1]	date of birth
usual address [1]	marital status
type of accommodation	relationship in household [3]
tenure	usual address one year ago
number of rooms	country of birth
availability bath/WC	long–term illness [2]
central heating [2]	ethnic group [2]
number of cars or vans	term–time address of students [2]
	economic/employment status
Note	hours worked per week [3]
[1] not processed, though	occupation [3]
postcodes included	industry of occupation [3]
[2] not included in 1981	address of workplace
[3] 10% returns coded	means of travel to work [3]
	higher education qualifications [3]
Source: Littler (1991)	Welsh language (Wales only)

The following topics provide useful information for assessment of housing need:

Concealed families
Lone parent and couple concealed families (with and without children) by the age of the family head and the age of the head of the main household.

Sharing households/not self contained accommodation
The number and type of household spaces in shared dwellings. Information is also available on tenure of households in non self–contained accommodation and household composition (See example from Hammersmith & Fulham table below).

Overcrowding
The number of households living at a density of more that one person per

room, which is generally accepted as a rough indicator of overcrowding, by tenure and household composition.

Housing standards
Lack of or sharing of bath/shower, WC and, for the first time, central heating by tenure and household composition.

Tenure
Information on tenure of both dwellings and households as well as separate analyses of pensioners, students (for the first time the term address of students is also given) and visitors.

Vacant homes
The total number of vacant dwellings. The vacant dwellings in the private sector can be calculated by subtracting known voids in local authority and housing association stock from the totals. The Census gives figures on whether dwellings appeared to be vacant because they were brand new, undergoing improvement, or some other reason. The latter figures are based on the *opinion* of the enumerators.

Ethnic Origin
This question is new to the Census. (Country of birth was asked in previous Censuses and used as an indicator of ethnic origin but that approach proved unsatisfactory.) Ethnic origin statistics can be used to provide information on local concentrations of ethnic groups, their age distribution and household composition and can be related to housing tenure.

Long–term illness
Information (for the first time) on individuals whose activities are limited by long–term illness or handicap covering such areas as their housing conditions, geographic concentrations etc.

Proxy for income
Data on household composition, economic activity, social class and car ownership may be used as broad indicators of relative income levels. The census does not provide information on incomes.

Mapping of Census data
When analysing Census information at ward or enumeration level it is possible for this data to be provided on a map. These maps are most useful in that they can illustrate areas of particular deprivation or potential renewal areas.

Hammersmith and Fulham (2) – Using the Census
Housing: Amenities and Overcrowding

Percentage of Households

	Lack or share use of bath/shower and/or inside WC		Exclusive use of bath/shower and/or inside WC		At over 1.0 persons / room	Total House-holds
	With CH	*No CH*	*With CH*	*No CH*		
H&F	1.1	2.6	72.9	23.3	4.9	69,823
Inner London	*1.2*	*2.1*	*77.9*	*18.8*	*5.6*	*1,096,141*
Outer London	0.9	0.9	81.8	16.5	3.2	1,667,025
Greater London	*1.0*	*1.4*	*80.2*	*17.5*	*4.1*	*2,763,166*
H&F 1981	15.2		84.8		7.5	61,057

Notes: the 1981 population base excludes households wholly absent on Census night. Source of 1981 data: Greater London County report (OPCS 1982). CH = Central Heating

In terms of measures of housing amenities used in previous Censuses, the housing in the Borough has continued to improve. In 1991, only 3.7% of households lacked or shared the use of a bath or shower and/or a WC. This compared to a figure of 15.2% in 1981 and represents a greater rate of improvement than for Inner London as a whole, though the Hammersmith and Fulham 1991 figure of 3.7% is marginally above the Inner London average of 3.3%.

In 1991, 4.9% of households lived at over 1.0 persons per room. This has reduced from 7.5% in 1981. The figure is below the Inner London average (5.6%) but above that for Greater London (4.1%).

8.5 Housing Supply

Data on the supply of housing is an important variable in establishing the imbalance of housing provision. Useful sources are as follows:

New housebuilding

Starts and completions by tenure are published for local authority districts in "Local Housing Statistics" (published quarterly by HMSO) containing information from housebuilders, housing associations on future development plans.

Relets

Housing departments should have information on local authority relets such as scale, location and type of dwelling. It is becoming increasingly important to consider housing association relets. Information may be obtained from housing associations themselves, or can be obtained from HAR10 forms which associations must submit to the Housing Corporation / Scottish Homes / Tai Cymru.

Chapter 9
Conclusion:
Housing Needs Assessments
– "Only The Beginning"

9.1 Introduction

Local housing needs assessments involve the drawing together of all available data on housing need and supply, as well as the collection of additional, new data from housing need surveys. To inform the authority's housing strategy and to formulate defensible affordable housing policies in local plans, it is important to examine the balance between supply and demand in the affordable housing sector, and the extent to which it can be met by homes for sale on the open market. An assessment of housing need is the starting point of a housing authority's strategic and enabling role. This final chapter considers some of the key aspects of housing needs assessments and makes suggestions to both central and local government regarding this crucial exercise.

9.2 No Standard Model

The standardisation of housing needs assessments is neither a feasible nor a desirable option. Each local authority must undertake the assessment according to the circumstances prevailing in its area eg. whether it is urban or rural etc. The components of an assessment also depend on the information which the authority has available, as well as the resources it is able to commit to such an important area of its work. There are however certain categories and sources of information which all local authorities should consider in carrying out a housing need assessment (see Chapter 4).

Although it is accepted that a standard model is not desirable, it would be very helpful for all concerned if the Government would provide some guidelines to ensure that the quality of the information derived from surveys is of an acceptable standard and that all local authorities' needs assessments may be comparable, particularly if this information is to be taken into account in Government department s' discretionary allocation of funds for housing.

9.3 Significant Resources

The collection of data for housing needs assessment requires significant use of resources, either in staff time or consultants' fees, for the analysis of the information gathered so that a comprehensive, and comprehensible, picture of the local housing situation can be produced. A household survey is only one element of housing needs assessment and in itself is likely to require considerable further work in order to make the most of the information obtained. The work to produce a detailed picture of need is only just beginning when a survey is undertaken and the data collected.

The task of drawing up a picture of housing need is crucial to the local authority's role as a strategic and enabling housing authority and should be recognised as such by local authorities in the allocation of resources as it is the foundation on which a strategy is built and implemented. Without a robust and wide–ranging assessment of need, a local authority's housing strategy is unlikely to be truly effective and efficient. Investment decisions made without such data may exacerbate inequalities in housing provision.

As housing strategies must now encompass the entire housing situation in their area, there is a strong argument for the funding of a survey, and any other strategic analysis and related work on the wider housing situation, to be provided from the General Fund. It is not equitable that only current local authority tenants should pay (through the HRA) for a service which will also be to the benefit of others.

If the Government believes the assessment of need to be as important as its guidance implies, it should make capital funding available for local authorities to undertake accurate assessments of need.

9.4 Prioritising Need

Given the shortage of funding available for housing investment compared to the scale of need, local authorities should have a comprehensive picture of housing need to enable them to ensure that, in prioritising need, all the problem areas are considered. In its publication on housing strategies, the Audit Commission (1992) provides some guidance on option appraisals and cost/benefit measures which enable local authorities to establish the option which will ensure the best "value for money" and thereby determine the housing strategy. However it stresses that local authorities must be clear where their priorities lie, as cost/benefit measures and option appraisals should only be considered for meeting priority needs. Guidance from the Scottish Office (1993) on *Strategic Priorities and Option Appraisal in Housing Investment* is also highly relevant in this context.

9.5 The Corporate Approach

Much emphasis is being placed on the "corporate" approach within local government. The need for such an approach in the delivery of services is highlighted by the Local Government Review which in many areas will bring together several local councils establishing a single unified authority. Housing needs assessments are instrumental in drawing together departments to consider the housing situation in the authority. Not only should such an exercise involve the housing, planning and social services departments, but should also involve the Council's solicitor, the Chief Executive's Office and others.

All these players can be involved, even if indirectly, in the formulation of the authority's housing strategy which may not have been the case previously. This process will result in the whole council having a far clearer understanding of housing issues which is likely to affect the way other departments carry out their respective tasks, giving greater consideration to housing need and how it might be met.

9.6 Publicising the Information

It is important, once the data on housing need is gathered and analysed and a comprehensive picture of the need in the area is available, that the local authority make the results as widely known as possible. A separate report on housing need may form part of the authority's Housing Strategy Statement or Housing Plan submitted to the DoE / Scottish Office / Welsh Office, but this is likely to be a detailed and technical document and will probably not be sufficiently accessible to others.

The information on housing need, particularly if a housing need survey has been undertaken, should be made available to other departments, other authorities (especially social services and planning) and voluntary organisations involved in housing provision most of which will have been consulted prior to the needs assessment exercise. Housing associations as the major providers of new affordable housing should be provided with detailed information which will inform their development programme for future years. Housebuilders, too, are likely to find the data of benefit. Information on the need for specific house types, for example, and on "affordability" in the local market will inform their business strategies. Enabling strategies are more likely to succeed if the delivery agencies are made aware of local need.

9.7 Updating Assessments

Housing need and supply are constantly changing. This factor will necessitate a regular, probably annual, review of needs assessment. However, not all aspects require to be revised each year. For example, a housing needs survey, given the cost and time implications (not to mention the likelihood of response rates decreasing) is unlikely to be repeated each year. Consideration will need to be given to repeating the exercise every three or five years, at least, as migration occurs, economic circumstances change and people's perceptions and aspirations alter.

Other aspects of the overall picture can be more regularly updated (eg house prices, waiting lists, homelessness data, new data at national/regional level) to ensure that the local housing strategy, which is revised each year, remains relevant to address changing needs and priorities.

References & Further Reading

ACRE (1993)
Enabling Rural Social Housing. ACRE.

Aldbourne Associates (1992)
Report of a Housing Need Survey for Christchurch Borough Council and Twynham Housing Association. Unpublished.

Aldbourne Associates (1992)
Report on a Housing Needs Survey for Llanelli Borough Council. Unpublished.

Audit Commission (1992)
Developing Local Authority Housing Strategies. HMSO, London.

Audit Commission (1991)
Numbers that Count, making good use of the 1991 Census, Information Papers Number 7. HMSO, London.

Brady et al (1991)
The Housing Needs of Single People in Harrogate. Policy Research Unit, Leeds Polytechnic for Harrogate Borough Council. Unpublished.

Bramley G (1991)
Bridging the Affordability Gap in 1990. ADC/HBF, London

Bramley G and Lambert C (1991)
Housing Needs and Affordability in East Cambridgeshire – Report of an initial feasibility study for East Cambridgeshire District Council. University of Bristol, School for Advanced Urban Studies. Unpublished.

Clark D and Dunmore K (1991)
Involving the Private Sector in Rural Social Housing.ACRE.

Cook S. (1993)
A Housing Officer's Concerns. Speech to a Care in the Community Seminar, St Edmundsbury Borough Council. Unpublished.

DCA Ltd (1992)
Ryedale Housing Needs Study – Enabling Report. Unpublished

Department of the Environment (1980)
Housing Requirements. HMSO, London.

Dunmore, K (1992)
Planning for Affordable Housing. HBF and IoH.

Fraser, R. (1991)
Working together in the 1990s. IoH.

Howes et al (1989)
Local Housing Needs in Cotswold Villages – A research report for the Cotswold District Council. Countryside and Community Research Unit of the School of Environmental and Planning Studies, Gloucestershire College of Art and Technology. Unpublished

Institute of Housing (1992)
Housing – the first priority. IoH White Paper.

Kleinman et al (1993)
Housing Needs in Cambridge – A study of Housing Needs and Provision in Cambridge 1991–2006, for Cambridge City Council. Property Research Unit, Department of Land Economy, University of Cambridge.

Littler S (1991)
The 1991 Population Census Preliminary Results and Planned Outputs for Wales. Welsh Housing Quarterly, Winter 1991.

London Borough of Hackney (1992)
Housing Strategy Statement 1993/94.

London Borough of Hammersmith and Fulham (1992)
Census 1991 Report. LBHF.

London Research Centre (1989)
The London Housing Survey 1986/7. LRC, London.

London Research Centre (1986)
The Housing Needs Survey: A comprehensive method of assessing housing requirements. LRC, London.

London Research Centre (1992)
Survey of Special Housing Needs in Bath and Wansdyke, for Bath City Council and Wansdyke District Councils. Unpublished.

Munroe et al (1993)
Best Practice Guidance for Local Market Analyses. Scottish Homes.

National Federation of Housing Associations and Office for Public Management (1992)
Assessment of Housing Requirements of People with Special Needs over the next decade. NFHA.

New Forest District Council (1992)
Housing Strategy Statement 1993/4.

NFHA/AMA/ADC (1993)
Social Housing Agreements. NFHA, London.

OPCS (1988)
The OPCS Disability Survey. HMSO, London

Parker J. (1993)
Taking Stock: a guide to local housing assessment. Housing Management Advisory Panel, Wales

Scottish Development Department (1977)
Scottish Housing Handbook 1: Assessing Housing Needs – A Manual of Guidance. Glasgow.

Scottish Office (1993)
Strategic Priorities and option Appraisal in Housing Investment. Scottish Office/Pieda, Edinburgh.

Smith M.E.H. (1989)
Guide to Housing, Third Edition. Housing Centre Trust.

Tai Cymru/Housing for Wales (1992)
Investment Policies and Plans 1992/3. Tai Cymru.

Watson L (1992)
Housing Care and Support in the New Forest District. New Forest Special Needs Housing Forum.

Watson L and Harker, M (1993)
Community Care Planning: A Model for Housing Need Assessment. IoH / NFHA, London.

Whitehead, C and Kleinman, M (1992)
A review of housing needs assessments. Housing Corporation.

Williams et al (1991)
Evaluating the Low Cost Rural Housing Initiative. DoE, London.